How to Succeed as an Entrepreneur in Ghana
A Practical Guide

Adonis & Abbey Publishers Ltd/Skylark Publications (Ghana)
St James House
13 Kensington Square,
London, W8 5HD
United Kingdom

Website: http://www.adonis-abbey.com
E-mail Address: editor@adonis-abbey.com

Nigeria:
Suites C4 & C5 J-Plus Plaza
Asokoro, Abuja, Nigeria
Tel: +234 (0) 7058078841/08052035034

British Library Cataloguing-in-Publication Data
A catalogue record for this book is available from the British Library

ISBN: 978-1-909112-94-0

How to Succeed as an Entrepreneur in Ghana
A Practical Guide

John Kuada

Contents

Acknowledgement

The motivation for writing this book comes mainly from owners of small businesses in Ghana who have spoken with me during management training sessions and workshops in the past three decades. They have repeatedly drawn my attention to the lack of practical guidelines that will help new business owners improve the performance of their companies and remain confident and determined in the face of adversities. This is a daunting task and this book is an initial response to this appeal. It seeks to provide Ghanaian entrepreneurs with some suggestions and pointers at sources of solutions to the challenges that they are likely to face. I am grateful to all the managers whose experiences have provided me with inspiration and insight into the way businesses are run in Ghana.

Chapter 1

Your Mindset is the First Key to Your Success

Introduction

Successful people are keenly aware that no human being can have everything he or she wants. But everyone can have what really matter to them if they work really hard for a really long period of time. I share this viewpoint and believe that we all have the potential within us to be achievers. The starting point is the determination within us to nurture our potentials and to bring about real change. When the determination is there, everything else begins to move in the direction that we desire. The moment you resolve to be an achiever, every nerve and fibre within your body immediately orients itself towards your success. The desire to start a business may be driven by such a determination – the determination to make a difference rather than barely survive. Most business people see achievement as more important than material or financial reward. Achievement gives them greater personal satisfaction than receiving praise or recognition. They regard financial reward as a measurement of success, not an end in itself.

This book is intended for those of you who have cultivated the inner desires to grow your businesses and to use the results of your efforts to make a real difference in your own lives and those of hundreds or even thousands of people within and outside Ghana. It narrates stories of those Ghanaians that have successfully grown their businesses and have made notable contribution to society as business people. It also provides guidelines that can help you succeed and offers insights into some of the challenges that you are likely to face.
Agambire and Agams Holding Company[1]

---

[1] Information presented in the book about Agambire and Agams Holdings is from various Internet Sources. See https://en.wikipedia.org/wiki/Roland_Agambire;

Let us start with the story of Mr Roland Agambire, one of Ghana's celebrated entrepreneurs of today. Mr Agambire has been described by some journalists as a personification of determination and he describes himself as a born entrepreneur. His story started as that of any other Ghanaian "village boy". Born in Sirigu, a farming community in northern Ghana, as one of 50 children to a father with ten wives, his background and challenges in early childhood became a source of determination for him to turn his life around. But he hardly expected the achievement that he has been able to record before turning 40. As a child he slept with ten of his siblings on the same mat, "like prisoners in a crowded jail", he recalls. His entrepreneurial talent manifested itself before he turned ten. He noticed that when the older men got drunk, they became careless with their money, dropping some of the coins in their pockets. The young Roland therefore decided to make the collection of coins his business. He went from one drinking spot to the other, looking for coins that might have fallen out of the pockets of the customers. This enabled him to "earn" his own pocket money while going to school. His next move was to use his savings to start producing and selling snacks to his school mates. This quickly turned into trading in essential household items such as kerosene. Since his village was close to the Burkina Faso border, he decided to cross the border with kerosene and cigarettes – items that were in a shorter supply in the border towns. This was the beginning of his export business. By the mid-1990s, his trading activities had expanded and he dabbled in cash crops exportation.

Today Roland Agambire is the CEO of Agams Holdings comprising eleven integrated companies. He is also the Chairman and CEO of RLG Communications Group (a leading ICT company), employing more than 500 permanent staff and 10,000 casual workers with an annual turnover of about two billion US dollars. Agams Holdings has interests in oil, construction, computing and

http://www.rlgglobal.com/AGAMS-Holdings;
http://eataghana.com/2016/08/13/biography-of-roland-agambire-ceo-of-rlg-and-agams-holdings;http://www.marcopolis.net/agams-holdings-building-a-legacy-in-african-ict-sector.htm - All retrieved on 9 January, 2017

telecommunications, financial services and trading. In 2012, Agambire's RLG was ranked the second best company in Ghana by the Ghana Investment Promotion Centre. In January 2013, the Pan African Television Network, E-TV voted him "the Most Influential Ghanaian for the year 2012" in a poll it conducted among its viewers. He was also voted "the Entrepreneur of the Year 2012" in a competition organised by the Entrepreneur Foundation of Ghana.

How can we explain Mr Agambire's extraordinary achievement? The starting point of all human achievements is the type of mindset one cultivates as one grows into adulthood. In her book *Mindset: The New Psychology of Success* Stanford psychologist Carol Dweck (2006) informs us that our views about our own abilities and potential (both conscious and unconscious) fuel our behaviour in life and predict our success. She argues that some people are guided overwhelmingly by a *fixed mindset*. A fixed mindset assumes that our character, intelligence, and creative ability are static givens which we cannot change in any meaningful way. In contrast, some people seem to have a *growth mindset*. This growth mindset is based on the belief that our basic qualities can be cultivated through our own efforts. This means those with a growth mindset will thrive on challenges and will experience failure as a springboard for growth.

Mr Agambire cultivated a growth mindset from early childhood. As a child he strongly felt that he deserved a lot more in life than his family background appeared to have dictated, and he was determined not to be a slave to his destiny. As the American writer Debbie Millman states, *"if you imagine less, less will be what you undoubtedly deserve"*. The determination to change one's destiny provides the inner motivation to live one's life with curiosity and a high level of attentiveness as one goes through life. These are important personality traits that successful entrepreneurs exhibit. Successful business people are therefore described as people with a strong desire for autonomy, independence, creativity, and tolerance of ambiguity, moderately risk-loving, and the determination to win. Societies that emphasise these attributes in the upbringing of their children will have many young people turn out to be entrepreneurs. It has also been noted that formal education may not be necessary for starting a new business. Many high school and college dropouts have become successful entrepreneurs throughout history.

Building on the above understanding, one can argue that the Ghanaian culture is not always helpful in nurturing entrepreneurial talents. A Ghanaian sociologist, Professor Assimeng (1981) describes the Ghanaian personality as characterized by:

1. Conformity and blatant eschewing of individual speculations
2. Unquestioning acquiescence
3. Lack of self-reliance, owing to the pervading influence of the extended family system
4. Fetish worship of authority and charismatic leaders
5. Hatred for criticism

These characteristics clearly constrain individual initiatives and entrepreneurial zeal. Seen against this background, Mr Agambire's achievements are extraordinary and an indication of the strength of his personality. Naturally, he has been described as a 'man of action'. Most successful entrepreneurs agree that comfort is a major constraint to success. You need to strive always to go beyond your comfort zone in order to be successful in any endeavour in life. Seeking comfort leads to an acceptance of mediocre performance. You may not be the smartest guy in Ghana. But that does not matter. If you multiply all your actions by ten you will definitely out-compete all others within your line of business. Once you get moving, you ride with the momentum. Consistent action allows entrepreneurs to gain knowledge and experience fast.

The latest addition to Mr Agambire's blossoming empire is the Hope City project which is estimated to be something in the region of US$10 billion. The Hope City, when completed, will have provided offices, accommodation for more than 50,000 people and will also host some of the tallest buildings on the continent. And this is not going to be the end. Mr Agambire has taken actions in other fields of endeavour as well. Despite his business success, he has been eager to study. He has taken courses in export and marketing offered by the Ghana Export Promotion Council. He has also completed a bachelor degree in business administration at the Ghana Institute of Management and Public Administration (GIMPA).

Mr Agambire was reported to tell the American business magazine, *Forbes*, that poverty is a perception. "It is the mind that changes the human being",[2] he observed. Thus, regardless of how small one's beginning might be, with hard work and the right thinking you would end up being what you always envisaged being", he added. It is important to bear in mind that poverty is more than just a lack of income. It also connotes lack of respect, self-worth, dignity, inclusion, choice and security. Poverty makes people resign to their living conditions and holds their creativity in check. Thus, poverty sets a negative spiral in motion. This means any effort made to alleviate poverty is itself growth-propelling since it unleashes hitherto untapped psychological and physical human resources within a community and thereby helps transform a negative spiral into a positive one. Poverty alleviation is therefore not a philanthropic project but a viable business proposition.

Having an Attentive Mindset

Most writers suggest that the entrepreneurial process starts with the "discovery" of opportunities. The discovery is usually done by alert individuals who are at all times scanning the horizon, as it were, ready to make discoveries. If we look closely into the Ghanaian economy today, there are numerous opportunities to do business and the very attentive individuals identify these opportunities and explore them – some successfully. This is also true for many other African countries. All economic analysts agree that there is a growing middle income group in nearly all African countries. Out of the 54 countries, 24 of them more than doubled their per capita income over 1990–2010. Household spending in Africa is projected to increase from $860 billion in 2008 to $1.4 trillion in 2020 (McKinsey, 2010) Furthermore, Africa's population is likely to grow to two billion

---

[2] See http://www.modernghana.com/news/490266/1/rlgs-roland-agambire-an-inspiration-to-ghanaian-yo.html

11

people and account for 20% of the world's population by 2050. As a whole, African consumers have remained underserved and underserviced and are waiting for attentive and hard-working business owners to serve them.

Psychologists have always reminded us that paying attention is a disciplined art. It requires taking time to observe from a variety of perspectives. Attentive individuals are able to discern the unfamiliar in the familiar, as well as the familiar in the unfamiliar.

Once again, Mr Roland Agambire's story illustrates this quite well. RLG had a modest beginning as a company. It started as Roagam Links in March 2001, repairing mobile phones, thereby serving the emerging needs of urban Ghanaians most of whom had acquired mobile phones for the first time. After successfully increasing RLG's market share by repairing mobile phones, the company began manufacturing them in 2008. Today, RLG assembles laptop computers, tablets, electronic notebooks, LCD television monitors, mobile handsets and various other types of communications equipment. In collaboration with Ghana's Ministry of Youth and Sports, RLG has established a training programme that aims to teach ICT-related disciplines to 30,000 young Ghanaians.

> *"The range of what we think and do is limited by what we fail to notice. And because we fail to notice that we fail to notice, there is little we can do to change; until we notice how failing to notice shapes our thoughts and deeds"* R.D. Laing
>
> *See*
>
> *https://www.brainyquote.com/quotes/quotes/r/rdlaing130951. html*

Mr Agambire sees himself as a visionary Ghanaian entrepreneur. He was quick to realise that Ghana needed to introduce its youth to the intricacies of ICT and train them to take advantage of its economic potential. As he explains, "I had a vision regarding the potential of developing ICT in Africa… It is not just about touching a computer and printing a document. The devices, the software and the overall supporting technology offer vast opportunities, and young Africans are starting to understand the possibilities behind these technologies."

Reflecting on the evolution of RLG, Mr Agambire noted in an interview that "the perception of the people was a key determinant in the company's success". He has encouraged his staff to be observant and take notes of how consumers respond to their products and service offerings. As he explained it, "we had to show Ghanaian people that our products were not just local. They are certified to international standards, and when people use an RLG product, the way it feels and functions is no different from that of renowned products from the United States or Europe."

Cultivate a Fighting Spirit

The achiever mindset builds a tenacity of character. Commitment and tenacity enable people to try something bold. Conventional wisdom teaches us that anything worth having is worth striving for with all one's might. It is also often said that if you are succeeding in everything you do, then you are probably not pushing yourself hard enough. You may risk failure when you do so. But you will not learn anything of value if you do not fail or know how to handle your failures.

"Every great success has always been achieved by fight. Every winner has scars....The men who succeed are the efficient few. They are the few who have the ambition and will-power to develop themselves. So choose to be among the few today."

Chris Kirubi – a Kenyan entrepreneur

Successful entrepreneurs need to learn to manage their failures. The owner and executive director of another well-known Ghanaian company, Nana Owusu-Afari of the Afariwaa Group of Companies, knows this well. He started his entrepreneurial journey in 1970, as "hobby" poultry farmer. The poultry farm was located at his backyard, in Tema. The success he enjoyed from the farm encouraged him to quit his job in 1976 and to move the farm onto a leased parcel of farmland from the Tema Development Corporation. He was willing to sacrifice the comfort that regular incomes provide and accept the uncertainties that start-ups bring with them. Today the Afariwaa Group of Companies has varied interests in farming, real estate development, veterinary pharmaceuticals, bottled water processing and production. It also has substantial shareholding in a couple of local banks. In a recent interview, Nana Owusu-Afari reflected on this journey and said, "The path to success, as a private sector operator, has not always been easy. It takes grit, a healthy sense of self-confidence, and an equally healthy dose of nationalistic fervour to traverse the turbulent and rough terrain of growing a business from start-up, through early stages of growth to a well-established business that is capable of surviving on its own strength".

It is also often said that 'adversity is a blessing in disguise'. Every failure teaches the successful individual what must be avoided in the future. It also develops fortitude and courage. To John Maxwell the author of the *Failing Forward*, "the difference between average people and achieving people is their perception of, and response to

14

failure". To him, failure is simply a price we pay to achieve success. Thus, when achievers fail, they see it as a momentary event, not a lifelong epidemic. His argument is that how people see failure and deal with it impacts every aspect of their lives. He therefore urges every person to learn to "fail forward". That is, we must accept failure as part of progress, challenge out-dated assumptions that guide our actions, take new risks and persevere, irrespective of previous negative outcomes.

- *Embrace adversity and make failure a regular part of your life. If you're not failing, you're probably not really moving forward.*

- *The next time you find yourself envying what successful people have achieved, recognize that they have probably gone through many negative experiences that you cannot see on the surface.*

John Maxwell (Author of Failing Forward)

John Maxwell suggests that there are seven key abilities that allow people to take each setback in life as a springboard to success. We can take an inspiration from these as a good starting point in our discussions of how to succeed as an entrepreneur in Ghana. The seven abilities are as follows:

1. **Reject rejection.** He argues that successful people do not blame themselves when they fail. They take responsibility for each setback, but they do not take the failure personally.

2. **View failure as temporary.** Rejection of failure means, in effect, that when people fail, they view their failures as temporary. That is, they do not personalise their failures or see their problems as holes they are permanently stuck in.

3. **View each failure as an isolated incident.** Seeing each failure as a temporary (rather than permanent) condition of life also means that each setback is just a small part of the whole and an opportunity to learn what not to do.

4. **Have realistic expectations.** High achievers are constantly aware that success takes time. In other words, there are going to be bumps along the way when you are aiming at something worthwhile.

5. **Focus on strengths.** Experience has shown that high achievers focusing on leveraging and amplifying their strengths rather than feel constrained by their weaknesses. The focus on strengths rather than weaknesses allows people to multiply their results.

6. **Vary approaches.** Achievers explore alternative solutions to every challenge they face and select what appears to them to be the most appropriate under given circumstances. But they are willing to vary their approaches to the problems they face. They do not repose a blind faith in any given approach. Maxwell advises that if one approach appears not to work for you, if it brings repeated failure, then try something else. The understanding here is that what works for another person may not necessarily work for you.

7. **Bounce back.** Finally, successful people are resilient. They don't let one error keep them down. They learn from their mistakes and move on.

Chapter 2

Make Profits for a Purpose

Introduction

Apart from your general mindset and attitude to life, it is important for you to think about the type of entrepreneur you want to be and the vision you have for your business. There are some of you who may see your business as a "survival workshop". That is, you enter into business out of sheer necessity. You would have loved to be a salaried employee if you had an opportunity to get a job. Your business therefore becomes a temporary occupation or a source of refuge. There may be others among you who are fortunate to have salaried jobs and therefore see your businesses as sources of supplementary incomes. If you fall into one of these two groups of people, you are not likely to look for opportunities to grow your businesses. But some of you may see the businesses as fetching more income than you initially expected and therefore begin to devote increasing amounts of time and resources to them. Your visions for the businesses will then change, and you will be willing to consider growth strategies.

If you are not a survival entrepreneur, you may have a higher goal for your business endeavours right from the beginning. You may reflect on the following questions: What should be the overriding vision of my business? If I want to be rich, what value do I aim at creating with my wealth? This chapter provides you with some ideas to help you reflect on these issues and take a stand that will guide your vision and mission for the business.

The Meaning in Your Life and Your Business

David W. Johnson the author of *Reaching Out* reminds us that life is characterised by an on-going search for both daily bread and daily meaning. The primary determinant of meaning in life is other people. Our lives are shaped by relationships we share with others and the relationships of thousands of other people. Human beings are therefore described as social animals. For many people, living purposefully means staying focused, not only on what is important for oneself, but on what creates value and makes life meaningful for others as well. This is also true for business ventures. Business performances are therefore no longer measured only in terms of profit. Elkington (2004) coined the term Triple Bottom Lines (TLP) to draw attention to the higher goals of businesses. The triple bottom lines are reflected in the 3Ps (profit, people and planet). That is, the performance of businesses must be concurrently assessed in terms of the impact of their operations on people within and outside the companies as well as the planet in general. In other words, companies must earn profits, because such profits are essential for further business growth and even survival. But earned profits should be reasonable, just, and not earned at the cost of various other stakeholders, especially not the community or the environment. Furthermore, companies operate through the actions of employees and provide their products and services to other people. As such, it is the responsibility of businesses to safeguard the interests of all persons that they relate directly to – i.e. within and outside the companies.

> *"From the standpoint of daily life, there is one thing we do know: that we are here for the sake of each other - above all for those upon whose smile and well-being our own happiness depends, and also for the countless unknown souls with whose fate we are connected by a bond of sympathy. Many times a day I realize how much my own outer and inner life is built upon the labours of my fellow men, both living and dead, and how earnestly I must exert myself in order to give in return as much as I have received." -*
> *Albert Einstein*

The world is now seeing the rise of a new kind of entrepreneur, who is determined to address the world's most pressing needs through business activities. This group of entrepreneurs tend to believe that they have an incredible opportunity to use their businesses as forces for good and make a tremendous difference in the world. They want to make profit for a purpose. You can be one of these persons.

Even if you have been pushed into business out of sheer necessity, you still have the potential to grow your business. It is a choice you have to make. As Steven Covey (the author of *The 7 Habits of Highly Effective People*) encourages us, "no matter how long we've walked life's pathway to mediocrity, we can always choose to switch paths". This means we all have the power to decide to live a *great* life - a life of an outstanding businessperson in Ghana. Thus, it is no longer enough for you, as a businessperson, to figure out how to make a profit. Money is still important, but you must not consider money as the be-all and end-all of business. You may see money as a tool to achieving another end – i.e. to fulfil a purpose. That is, you must make profit for a purpose. You must use the money you earn to fulfil your dreams of impacting the world in which you live. This may take the form of creating new job opportunities or helping other businesses to grow so that the communities in which you live prosper with you. Entrepreneurs that pursue social motives as integral parts of their businesses are also referred to as humanitarian or social entrepreneurs. They combine two fantastic and motivating aspects of business undertakings – i.e. the ability to do business and the ability to create social values. In other words, they turn corporate social responsibility into their core business.

Always remember the words of Anita Roddick, the founder of Body Shop "If you think you're too small to have an impact, try going to bed with a mosquito".

Some of you may be good at identifying business opportunities and providing innovative solutions to problems within your environment and therefore create viable business ventures out of these endeavours. Those of you who do so may also be growth-oriented. Growth-oriented entrepreneurs are usually described as those who can combine a strong desire for growth with the potential capacity to realise it.

Serving the Poor and Your Community for Profit and Purpose

Let me emphasise that businesses can and should create not just economic value, but also engage constructively with the community where they are located. As an entrepreneur, you may not get rich quickly but you will enjoy the satisfaction that social contributions provide. It is not always necessary for you to have a crystal-clear vision of who you are; what you want to do; and where you want to go before you start. It is enough to be guided by faith in the simple truth that you are in this world to be of value to mankind. As Dr Martin Luther King Jr. says, "take the first step in faith. You don't have to see the whole staircase. Just take the first step". This is a view adopted by most religious entrepreneurs. They believe that God (The Universe, Source, etc.) gave them unique talents and gifts for a specific reason. You are destined to create and serve others.

> *"Be the change that you wish to see in the world"*
> *– Mahatma Gandhi*

It is becoming evident in both developed and the developing world that great companies are not great just because they make lots of money. They make lots of money precisely because they are great. In Africa, the conventional marketing logic tends to consider many Africans as being too poor to be viable customers. Prahalad (2005) has a different perspective. He estimates that the poor people of the world have buying power equal to $8 billion per day. This makes the poor a multitrillion-dollar annual market on a global scale. Considering the fact that the African population is growing rapidly and is expected to be two billion within the next three decades, businesses can hardly afford to ignore even the poor segments of the population. Kotler and Lee (2009) convey the same perception when they argue that the poor have the right to want what the rich want and, as a group, they constitute an incipient demand waiting to be tapped.

Fred Swaniker

Some successful Ghanaian business owners are beginning to see the wisdom in this approach to business. They are keenly aware that it is not possible to do long-lasting business in this country without contributing in some significant manner to society. They see themselves as part of their social contexts, for better or for worse.

One of these types of young Ghanaian entrepreneurs is Fred Swaniker (born in 1976) to a Ghanaian magistrate (father) and educationist (mother). Before he turned 30, he had lived in four African countries (Ghana, Gambia, Botswana and Zimbabwe), attended Macalester College in Minnesota as well as Stanford School of Business (USA), worked for McKinsey & Company in South Africa, and established African Leadership Academy, African Leadership Network, Global Leadership Adventures and Africa Advisory Group. He was praised by Barack Obama and other prominent leaders for his entrepreneurial achievements. His motivation to start African Leadership Academy came from his reflections on the situation that wealthy African families send their children to the US and UK for good university educations. He wondered why Africa could not establish a top-notch school for African students in Africa. Drawing on his Silicon Valley connections he was able to raise funds to establish the Academy in 2004. In 2016 he opened the doors to his latest entrepreneurial ventures – The African Leadership University – in partnership with Scotland's Glasgow Caledonian University. The University's overriding goal is to train high-calibre leaders who will drive Africa's development and inspire generations to come. The University is currently located in Mauritius with the ambition of building 25 campuses across the continent and training three million leaders in five decades.

Robert Asare

Entrepreneurial visions do not emerge fully-formed overnight from the entrepreneur's head, but rather evolve over a span of time, following a period of exploration, talking to people, reading, reflecting, etc. One other prominent Ghanaian entrepreneur that demonstrates the "profit for purpose" orientation to entrepreneurship is Mr Robert Asare, the owner of Ghana Craft Company (name changed to preserve its anonymity).The idea of establishing Ghana Craft Company (GCC) was hatched in the mid-1980s when Robert Asare was then the CEO of the Ghanaian subsidiary of a major European company. He had always considered Ghanaian handicrafts to have distinctive features and therefore brought them as gifts for his European and North American friends on his business trips. For many years he had wondered why the sector had not grown into a viable industry that contributed substantially to economic growth and poverty alleviation in the country. For most artisans, the production of handicraft products had remained a hobby rather than a source of significant and sustainable income. This meant that they hardly showed commitment to their work and lacked motivation to upgrade their skills, let alone introduce new products. He believed he could help transform the sector through the use of his professional experience and business contacts.

In 1988, Robert Asare asked the marketing director of his former company, James Banor (who had also retired) to join him in building GCC into a strong intermediary for the handicraft sector. Together, they conducted some preliminary investigations to uncover the domestic and export opportunities for the best known handicraft products in the country. The information they gathered suggested that the economic policies initiated by the Ghanaian government in the mid-1980s were making positive contributions to the industry's growth. By the late 1980s, Ghana was acclaimed by the World Bank and other international economic monitors to be at the threshold of economic lift-off. There were increasing numbers of foreign visitors in the country, creating a healthy market for handicrafts. They reasoned that if the products were sold in convenient locations and were appropriately packaged tourists visiting Ghana would be willing to pay higher prices for them and this would help grow the sector. This reasoning let them to open souvenir shops close to major shopping centres in Accra, Tema and Kumasi. They reasoned further that the tourists would serve as windows to the export markets since their buying behaviour would be indicative of the preferences of potential consumers in the major European and North American countries.

The handicraft industry in Ghana has grown from these modest beginnings. In the 1990s the industry was estimated to be worth barely US$ 200,000 in annual sales. This has grown to a US$ 28-million industry by 2011. An estimated number of 50,000 handicraft producers now depend fully or partly on the sector for their livelihoods and 5,000 of them produce for the export market.

In 2005, a comprehensive training programme was initiated aimed at upgrading the production skills of the local artisans and raising their awareness of hazardous production methods. About two per cent of its earnings have been redistributed among the rural-based producers in the form of bonuses and provision of raw materials. Another 2 per cent are now spent on corporate social investments such as construction of school buildings and provision of other facilities to the primary schools in the major handicraft production regions.

The company has also established two "enhanced handicraft production centres" in Accra and Tamale to serve artisans in the southern and northern parts of Ghana, respectively. The centres are manned by six well-trained "master artisans" – three at each centre. Products bought from artisans in the rural areas were brought to the centre where the master artisans supervised younger apprentices to provide them with neater finishing touches before they were shipped to the market. The centres also provided training at substantially subsidized costs to local artisans that would like to improve their skills.

The Challenges of Socially Responsible Entrepreneurship

The "profit for purpose" vision may be a challenge for some of you due to the Ghanaian culture and the obligations imposed by our extended family systems. Business scholars who have studied the growth ambitions of Ghanaian entrepreneurs tend to agree that our family systems can sometimes be a drag on our economic efforts. Our business people are expected to spend their earnings on kinship obligations such as financing the studies of brothers, cousins, nephews and nieces, lodge newcomers (from rural areas arriving in the major towns to escape poverty), and finance the multitude of ceremonies that fill the Ghanaian social life.

I have discussed this issue at length with a number of Ghanaian entrepreneurs during the past three decades. Nearly all of them agree to the cultural constraints of succeeding as an entrepreneur in Ghana. One of the business owners I have talked to is the owner of Environmental Development Group (EDG), which started on a very small scale in Ho in the Volta Region. When the entrepreneur established his first business (a bakery) in the 1970s, he had to give it up due to conflicts with his cousin. When he started his second business, his dad asked him to employ some of his relatives, although they did not have the required business skills and experience. However, once they were employed it became extremely difficult to fire them, even those who were caught using business assets for their own personal purposes. The older relatives depended on him several years after their retirement, even after he had paid them their gratuity and other entitlements. "But what else can I do?" he asked inviting my understanding during my interview with him. He explained the situation further:

Our Ghanaian culture has inbuilt taken-for-granted birth-rights for family members. Many assume that it is their birth-right to have a share of the wealth of the relatively better-off members of their families without giving anything in return.... As a person, I am soft by nature. This makes it difficult for me to reconcile the needs of my business with the expectations of family members.

Some entrepreneurs have sought to address this problem in a creative (but unorthodox) manner. They simply decide to "de-link" themselves from the family while their businesses are young. Those entrepreneurs who deliberately disconnected themselves from their families came back to the family fold when their businesses had gained a stronger economic foundation and could withstand the predatory tendencies of their families. There may be some lessons to learn from these entrepreneurs.

Chapter 3

Grow Your Business

Introduction

Starting a new business is usually a decision that comes with excitement. But growing your business is another story. It is often said that being an entrepreneur is a marathon activity with lots of sprints. You may need to win a lot of little races, and this will provide you and your employees with momentum. Issues of prioritisation of your resources, including your time are important. How do you gain attention for you and your company – i.e. make your company known and significant? How do you gain more customers? How do you make sure that they become loyal to you? These are questions that you will continue to grapple with for many years. This chapter provides you with some tips on how to stay on the growth path right from the beginning of your entrepreneurial journey.

Be Focused

To succeed as an entrepreneur, you must focus your time, energy and financial resources on a single business. You must avoid establishing several small businesses that you run concurrently. Although you may think that you can reduce your risks of business collapse by diversifying your investments and income base, such a diversification at an early stage of your business life may become a source of a major setback. Spreading your capital and managerial time over many small activities means that none of these businesses receives the attention and resources it deserves in order to grow or survive during difficult times.

Some of you may be good at identifying business opportunities and providing innovative solutions to problems within your environment and therefore create viable business ventures out of these endeavours – i.e. you will be growth-oriented. Growth-oriented entrepreneurs are usually described as those who can combine a strong desire for growth with the potential capacity to realise it. Most writers on entrepreneurship agree that attributes that characterise growth-oriented entrepreneurs include tenacity, perseverance, persistency, determination, commitment, resilience, self-confidence, adaptability, flexibility, networking abilities and passion. These are coupled with an understanding of the needs of the market and the goods and services one seeks to offer. Certainly not all successful entrepreneurs have all these attributes at one go. Most people develop them as they gain experience with their business ventures.

Be Quick at Spotting Opportunities

To be a growth-oriented entrepreneur you need to be able to recognise an opportunity when you see one. Specifically, you need to be able to identify a problem or gap, and come up with an innovative solution. A popular anecdote frequently told to students at international business workshops goes like this: The management of a footwear company sent one of their salespersons to an African town. When he got there he immediately wrote back to his manager: "there is no market for our products here – no one uses footwear here". A competitor to the first company sent its salesperson to the same town. He, in turn, wrote back to his manager, "send a truck load of sandals – no one uses footwear here". This anecdote illustrates very well how two persons can perceive the same business environment differently.

The same idea holds true in Ghana. A quick look at the business environment will show that there are business opportunities all around. The question is to know where to look. Let us take one example. The domestic market for fruit juices has been growing strongly in recent years, in part, because Ghanaian consumers are showing increasing appreciation for the natural taste and health benefits of Ghana's own agricultural products. According to estimates, 10.4 million litres of fruit juice are consumed yearly. However, approximately 70% of the juice products are imported.

Ghana is endowed with an assortment of fruit, including mangoes, pineapples, citrus and coconut, among others. And we are often told that the country's location offers conditions that are close to optimum for growing tropical fruits. The opportunity to transform agricultural produce into juice and other value added consumer products for domestic and foreign markets and ultimately dominate the processed fruits industry exists, but few local companies have taken advantage of this opportunity.

The story of Danso Fruit Drinks (named changed to preserve anonymity) provides a good illustration of how some successful Ghanaian entrepreneurs capture opportunities. It was the first registered Ghanaian company to produce tropical fruit juice. It all started when the founder (Mr Charles Danso) attended an enterprise development seminar in 1985. This seminar entirely changed the direction of his life. One of the speakers at the seminar talked about the local fruit production and marketing system in Ghana at that time. He informed the participants that fruits and vegetables produced in Ghana were harvest-dependent seasonal products, available only during certain periods of the year, and had a limited storage life. Thus, the domestic market was usually glutted during the harvest season – prices were low and the post-harvest losses were very high. Consumers hardly got fresh fruits to buy for the rest of the year, and those which reached the market were sold at extremely high prices. Thus, year-round fruit consumption was a luxury that only the relatively rich consumers could afford. In his view, one of the supply-related challenges faced by the sector was to design a production system that could ensure a year-round production. Furthermore, the local fruit-processing industry was under-developed with only a handful of small-scale processing activities. Large volume fruit processing for the mass market did not exist. There was therefore a marketing gap that needed to be filled.

After the seminar Mr Danso became obsessed with the idea of creating his own business, and it should be in the fruit-processing industry. He decided to retire from his position as a bank manager. He was at the time in his early fifties. With all his children in their early 20s, he felt he could venture into new spheres of life with the uncertainties that come with entrepreneurial ventures.

The first challenge, in his view, was to set up a fruit-processing facility of a significant size and to find someone knowledgeable in fruits processing to handle the production. He would also need to organise the purchasing, transportation, and storage of fruits during the harvest seasons. He discussed his ideas with his uncle, Mr Alfred Amanea, a chemistry lecturer from the University of Ghana who had some working experience from the Ghana Standards Board (GSB). They agreed to establish the business together. They also agreed that it would be wise for the company to establish its own farms in order to reduce its dependence on the local fruits producers, since there were no recognised commercial fruits farms in the country at that time. This would help ensure a year-round supply of the fruits for the processing factory.

The company was established in 1987 and was named Danso Fruit Drinks (DFD). Danso was the name of a popular TV Evangelist in Ghana at that time. Although Mr Danso did not have any family relationship with the preacher, taking on the name provided the company and its products with unaided and instantaneous brand identification. But, at the same time, it conveyed an association of ethical probity.

Thus, DFD became a front-runner company in the cultivation, processing, and marketing of tropical fruit juice in Ghana. By 1995 the company had 5000 hectares of pineapple, 1000 hectares of orange and 300 hectares of mangoes under cultivation. Mr Danso became the majority shareholder with 60% of the equity. His uncle's contribution was 30% of the equity, while Mr Danso's wife, Catherine, bought 10% equity. In 2003, the company's farms had been expanded to 7000 hectares of pineapples, 5000 hectares of oranges, 2000 hectares of mangoes, 1000 hectares of papaya in addition to guava, passion fruit and a few other exotic tropical fruits cultivated on an experimental basis.

DFD started production of a small batch of pineapple juice in 1989. The product was sold in 1 litre Tetra Pak containers, mainly to the catering sector and to hotels in Accra. In 1992, it added mango and orange juice to its products. By 2003, the variety of tropical fruit juices produced by the company had increased to include papaya, guava, citrus, and various combinations of these fruits into different types of juices. Sales began to grow rapidly from 1995 when the company began to sell its products to the broader market segment in 200 ml Tetra Pak containers and changed its distribution system to serve this market segment.

> *"History has demonstrated that the most notable winners usually encountered heartbreaking obstacles before they triumphed. They won because they refused to become discouraged by their defeats"*
> - *B.C. Forbes*

Turn Problems into Opportunities

Going back to our mindset discussions in chapter one, it is important to stress once again that our mindset is a key determinant of how we see the world. It is often said that how we think about a problem is more important than the problem itself. In the same vein Albert Einstein argues that the significant problems we face in life cannot be solved at the same level of thinking we were when we created them. These perspectives on solving problems in daily life apply to business as well. Too often we focus on problems within our business environment and fail to see opportunities right in front of us. When you focus on your problems – when you only think of what is wrong – you will only see problems and fail to see opportunities and solutions. It is advisable to make conscious efforts to turn things around. Spend your time and energy finding solutions rather than worrying about the problems. Worries do not solve problems. There is a saying that "when you think of problems you will only attract more problems". Instead, when you think of solutions your brain cells will initiate a positive spiral - attracting solutions and opportunities. Even if you do not find immediate solutions to your problems, you will certainly cultivate a positive and confident attitude to them.

> *An optimist sees an opportunity in every calamity; a pessimist sees a calamity in every opportunity"*
>
> *– Winston Churchill*

You must learn to develop an optimistic mindset and attitude to life – seeing more opportunities than problems within the operational environment. Winston Churchill is quoted as saying *a pessimist is one who sees calamities in all new situations while an optimist is one who sees opportunities in all calamities.* But many Ghanaians tend to focus, too often, on problems in their immediate environments. In doing so, they fail to see opportunities right in front of them. So, a piece of good advice I will give you is this:start your day by focusing on finding opportunities and solutions rather than problems.

Exploiting opportunities entails a willingness to take some risk. Let me pass on a piece of advice I once received from a successful entrepreneur. He said, "Each day I try to do something I am a little not ready to do. I think that is how you grow. When there is that moment of 'Wow, I'm not really sure I can do this,' and you push through those moments, that is when you have a breakthrough."

It is often said that Ghanaians, by nature, avoid risk as managers. If you are such a person, you will be satisfied with small gains and will be less likely to try new ways of doing things until other people have proved these new ways as good. Your strategy will therefore be reactive rather than proactive. You will not make major gains, but you will also avoid major losses.

Ghanaians are also described as being short-term-oriented in their business decisions. This means they are more likely to place greater emphasis on short or quick gains, and emphasise leisure today rather working hard for major gains and pleasure in the distant future. If you have this kind of orientation to your business, you will not plough back much of your immediate earnings into your business and chances of your business growing will be constrained.

But, as noted above, do not run after every business opportunity that you may identify yourself or your employees may bring to your attention. You need to decide on what areas of business activity you would want to concentrate on. By focusing your resources on specific business activities you will be able to develop unique skills and capabilities that will allow you to compete more effectively and thereby grow your business. You will also be able to conserve enough resources to take advantage of good opportunities in the future.

Maintain Clear Intentions, Passion and Action

The management literature offers three guidelines for building growth-oriented entrepreneurial ventures (Kuada, 2016A). These are popularly described as **"the three C's of growth"**. They are:

1. **C**lear Intentions
2. **P**assionate **C**ommitment
3. **C**onsistent Action

The chances of making it big in business are remote if you do not have a clear intention. Words that are usually associated with intention include awareness, aspiration, proclivity, drive and commitment. The management gurus Hamel and Prahalad coined the concept "strategic intent" of business leaders in order to describe the importance of clear intentions. The concept *strategic intent* captures the essence of winning in business and sets a target that deserves personal effort and commitment. That is, it fosters a winner mindset not only in the owner of a business but among key employees, as well. This means that without a strategic intent you are likely to trim your ambitions to match your current resources and only spot opportunities that your immediate resources can capture. You will not stretch your imagination and find new solutions to existing problems if such solutions will require finding resources that you do not currently possess. Furthermore, you are not likely to identify opportunities that lie in the horizon or try to attain seemingly impossible goals.

Clear intentions must be backed by passion and commitment. Blending passion and commitment helps you remain focused. It also provides you the reason to work hard. It is often said that passion is the fuel that ignites individuals' desires to work hard. When you are passionate about what you are doing you will choose to make good use of every moment. You will see each day as an open opportunity for mastering skills and furthering your goals. Thus, when you have abundant passion you will undoubtedly experience success. And the more success you experience, the more you will increase your passion. In this way passion rewards itself. It is through consistent and diligent work, coupled with patience and flexibility, that you can climb the ladder of success.

Intention, passion and commitment may not get you to your goals without action. Action is therefore seen as the platform on which success rests. Action empowers you and enables you to create your own future. Benjamin Disraeli is quoted as saying "action may not always bring happiness; but there is no happiness without action." An action-oriented businessperson will always be proactive and will not wait for things to happen to him/her but rather let things happen. Stephen Covey (2004), the author of *The 7 Habits of Highly Effective People* writes, "our basic nature is to act, and not be acted upon. As well as enabling us to choose our response to particular circumstances, this empowers us to create our circumstances." (p.75). "Sustaining an audience is hard," Bruce Springsteen once said. "It demands a consistency of thought, of purpose, and of action over a long period of time". The cumulative results of our actions eventually create the circumstances that place us on the path of success. I admit that it is not possible to be action-oriented under all circumstances. When fate appears to be against you there may be the need to find means of energising yourself. A way to do this is to remind yourself consistently of your goals in life.

Pay Attention to Growth-Oriented Products and Services

A group of consultants in the United States of America - The Boston Consulting Group – once developed a model that classifies product classification in terms of "stars", "question marks", cash-cows" and "dogs". This model is reproduced in Figure 3.1 and provides a simple but useful overview of how companies can manage their product/service portfolios for sustained growth and profitability. I would like you to reflect on the guidelines in the model and learn from it (Kuada, 2016B).

"Stars" consititute a company's new/innovative products and services that provide values that its customers did not anticipate. They reflect the company's capacity to make decisions that explore opportunities that are barely incipient and therefore provide it with a first mover advantage. As long as the company can hold competitors off, it can establish itself effectively in that business area. It is, however, important to realise that such propositions are risky. The company is likely to be a pioneer in the specific line of business, and its potential customers many have no knowledge of how valuable the goods and services are. "Cash cows" are products and services that customers are familiar with and demand. This is an area where efficiency is highly important. Costs must be reduced, quality must be guaranteed, delivery systems and prices must be aligned to customer expectations and customer complaints (if they occur) must be handled swiftly and satisfactorily. "Question mark" products and services are also known as *problem children*. They are classified as such because they have shown disappointing performances on the market. "Dogs" are goods and services that are no longer in high demand and require the company to spend more to serve its customers than the customers are willing to pay. It is always advisable to phase out such products quickly or re-launch them as new ones to new target customers who will see them as a "star" of a kind.

Figure 3.1: The Boston Consulting Group Matrix

High	Question Marks	Stars

Market Growth		
Low	Dogs	Cash Cow

Low　　　High

Market Share

This matrix is a useful guide to how you can accelerate your growth by balancing investments between exploration of new ideas and business lines and exploitation of established lines of business to make profit. You must always remember that growth requires cash input to finance added assets; the quicker you want to grow your business, the more added cash you require. You can generate part of this cash from your existing line of business – i.e. your cash cow. The more successful you are doing in your existing line of business, the more money you will have to invest in growth related activities as long as you do not spend your profit frivolously. It is also important to remember that no line of business can grow indefinitely. You must therefore plan ahead and be on the lookout for high growth businesses. It is your ability to manage forward that will determine your prosperity as an entrepreneur.

Chapter Four

Design a Winning Strategy

Introduction

I have suggested earlier that in order to grow your business, you need to have a clear view of the nature of business you want to undertake and a well-defined sense of where you want your business to be in the next five to ten years. To this end, you need a strategy that will enable you to deliver a unique value to your customers and position yourself uniquely in your industry. But when you read the management literature, you will note that strategy is a word with many meanings and there is no agreement among management scholars about how this may be done. Some view it as a tool for implementing radical changes and creating a new vision of the future in which the company is a leader rather than a follower of trends set by others. Others see it as the determination of the basic long-term goals and objectives of an enterprise, and the adoption of courses of action and the allocation of resources for carrying out these goals. This chapter provides you with some ideas about how to understand the strategic process and how to design and implement a winning strategy.

The Concept of Strategy

The following three questions will help you in formulating your strategy: (1) where do you want your business to go – i.e. goals?; (2) how is your business going to get there – i.e. strategic actions?; and (3) how will you know when you get there – i.e. evaluation? The main emphasis of strategy is thus to enable an organisation to achieve competitive advantage with its unique capabilities by focusing on present and future direction of the business.

Characteristics of Strategy

Some scholars see strategy as a planned set of activities. That is, the process is supposed to start with the formulation of what leaders of the organisation "plan" to do, and then it is followed by the actions. This conventional understanding implicitly assumes a separation between those with the talent and skills to formulate strategies and those who implement them. Planned strategies therefore have two essential characteristics: (1) they are made in advance of the actions to which they apply, and (2) they are developed consciously and purposefully. Top executives are expected to play a key role in the planning process because they have the skills and broader overview of their organisations' vision and direction. The implementation falls in the laps of middle and lower level managers who have the skills and knowledge of specific (tangible and intangible) resources in different parts of their organisations to take the required actions and make adjustments, where necessary.

A strategic planning process consists of a series of steps. These are the most typical among them:

1. Establishing a mission statement and key objectives for the organisation.
2. Analysing the external environment (to identify possible opportunities and threats).
3. Conducting an internal organisational analysis (to examine its strengths and weaknesses and the nature of current management systems, competencies and capabilities).
4. Setting specific goals.
5. Examining possible strategic choices / alternatives to achieve organisational objectives and goals.
6. Adoption / implementation of chosen choices.
7. Regular evaluation of actions in terms of efficiency and effectiveness.

In contrast to a planning perspective on strategy, other scholars see strategy as a pattern in a stream of decisions. That is, to them, strategies need not be deliberately planned, but can emerge as patterns or consistencies in streams of decisions and behaviours which managers and other key employees take. Following this line of thinking, the strategic process can be broken into the following four distinct phases: namely - intended strategy, deliberate strategy, emergent strategy, and realised strategy. *Intended strategies* are plans conceived by the top management team. *Realised strategies* constitute those parts of the intended strategies that employees are able to implement. Some parts of the intended strategies may not be implemented, possibly because assumptions made in the intended strategy have been found not to hold in reality. *Emergent strategies* represent all the strategic decisions that emerge from the complex processes in which individual managers adapt to changing external circumstances and make modifications in the intended strategies. Thus, the realised strategy is a consequence of deliberate and emerging factors that influence companies' behaviour.

The understanding is that the process of assessing and adjusting the direction of a business in response to changes in its operational environment need not be carefully planned in advance for it to be called a strategy. As long as managers are clear about their companies' objectives and are alert about changes that might affect the attainment of these goals and take steps that consciously respond to these changes or initiate actions that improve their chances of success, they will be considered to be managing their companies strategically. Strategic management therefore means making conscious choices that respond to current situations or anticipate the environment in which their businesses will be operating in the future. It requires what may be aptly described as *strategic awareness.*

From a business perspective, emergent strategies tend to encourage continuous improvements in costs, product quality, new product development, manufacturing processes and distribution to fulfil customers' expectations. Marketing managers adopting emergent approaches to strategy formulation are more likely to excite their key customers by taking advantage of situations as and when they occur to go beyond the immediate expectations of these customers without undue extra costs. But this requires empowering salespersons to take initiatives in specific situations.

Most effective strategies tend to combine planning and control (deliberate strategies) with adaptation, flexibility and incremental learning. In other words, your company's actual strategy (its realised strategy) will most often be the outcome of the adaptation of a plan to emergent issues in the environment. This means the realised strategy can be very different from the strategy as planned.

Evaluation of Strategies

Whether one subscribes to the planning perspective or the strategic management perspective, it is important to bear in mind that strategy can be neither formulated nor adjusted to changing circumstances without a process of strategy evaluation. Whether performed by an individual or as part of an organisational review procedure, strategy evaluation forms an essential step in the process of guiding an organisation.

The process of strategy evaluation consists of the following steps:

1. **Specifying Performance Benchmark** - Benchmarking is the process of comparing one's business processes and performance to the best performance within an industry. It helps management to identify industry leadership performance targets. Alternatively, the company can decide on its own internal performance benchmark against which the success or failure of the strategy can be evaluated.
    When fixing the benchmark performance target, it is essential to discover the special requirements for performing the main tasks outlined in the strategy and the capabilities (including resources) to perform these tasks. The performance indicator that best identify and express the special requirements might then be determined to be used for evaluation. The organisation can use both quantitative and qualitative criteria for comprehensive assessment of performance. Quantitative

criteria may include determination of net profit, ROI, earning per share, cost of production, rate of employee turnover, etc. Among the qualitative factors are subjective evaluation of factors such as - skills and competencies, risk taking potential, flexibility, etc.

2. **Measurement of Performance -** The actual performance is then compared with the benchmark targets. In doing the performance measurement, the strategists must specify the acceptable degree of tolerance gap between the actual target and the accepted performance target.

3. **Analysing Variance** – If the analysis reveals gaps in the company's performance, it is important to analyse the variance – i.e. seek good explanations for the differences. The explanations may be found in changes in either the internal or the external environments. The positive deviation indicates a better performance but it is quite unusual always to exceed the target. The negative deviation is an issue of concern because it indicates a shortfall in performance. It is possible that negative deviations are simply due to overoptimistic targets, in the first place.

4. **Taking Corrective Action** – Corrective actions must be planned and taken to close the gap between actual performance and the targets. In situations where the performance is consistently less than the desired performance, the management may be required to carry out a detailed analysis of the factors responsible for such performance. If it happens that strategic goals have been too high, it may make sense to lower the targets.

It is often argued that the critical factors that impact performance may not be directly observable or may take a long time to be noticed. By the time they become noticeable, it may well be too late for an effective response. Thus, it is important for managers to look beyond the obvious facts regarding the short-term performance of a business when they evaluate the effectiveness of their strategies. They must instead appraise those more fundamental factors and trends that govern success in the long run. In this way, they are more likely to capture the hidden influencing factors in good time.

The management literature teaches that any strategy (planned or emergent) must also satisfy four broad criteria:

1. **Consistency**: The strategy must not present mutually inconsistent goals and policies.

2. **Consonance**: The strategy must represent an adaptive response to the external environment and to the critical changes occurring within it.

3. **Advantage**: Strategy must provide for the creation and/or maintenance of a competitive advantage in the selected area of activity.

4. **Feasibility**: The strategy must neither overtax available resources nor create insoluble problems.

Staying on Track with Your Strategy

The discussions above show that strategies will help you stay on track. This means your plan should be more than just a document that lives in a drawer all year. You should use it as a way to check in each month to compare what you are doing within your business with how this is influencing your performance both in the short run and the long run. There are some simple things you need to do on a routine basis in order to stay on track without misusing your resources. Whenever you or your key employees want to take an action and commit resources, ask if the proposed actions make positive, neutral or negative contributions to the goals outlined in your strategy. In other words, will these actions get you closer to your goals or will they constitute distractions?

Chapter Five

Managing Efficiently and Effectively

Introduction

As a manager, you will be required to make several decisions that affect the profitability of your company. Two main management concepts that you must bear in mind in these decisions are *efficiency* and *effectiveness*. Many managers find these two concepts rather confusing since they are frequently used interchangeably in everyday language. But if you understand their differences, this will help you in evaluating each decision in terms of how they will influence the profitability, growth and sustainability of your business. This chapter provides some clarity in the definition and usage of the concepts and explains their implications for management decisions.

Efficiency

The term *efficiency* is used in management to refer to the measurement of relationship between inputs and outputs, or how successfully inputs have been transformed into outputs in an organisation. In simple language, efficiency refers to doing things in a right manner – i.e. obtaining maximum output with minimum resources. Economists use the term "economic efficiency" to cover three sub-classifications of efficiency – productive efficiency, technical efficiency and dynamic efficiency. Productive efficiency is achieved when output is produced at minimum cost. That is, if you use your resources in a productively efficient manner it means you use the least necessary inputs to produce a given output of any commodity or service. In other words, you are productively efficient. The concept of productive efficiency includes both technical efficiency and dynamic efficiency. Technical efficiency refers to the extent to which it is technically feasible to reduce any input without decreasing the output, and without increasing any other input in your production process. Dynamic efficiency refers to the allocation of resources over time, including allocations designed to improve economic efficiency and to generate more resources. Dynamic efficiency may therefore directly influence the long term survival of your business.

Effectiveness

The term *effectiveness* relates to the vision and mission that you have for your business – i.e. your dreams or what you desire to be the outcome of your business efforts. Effectiveness therefore measures the nature and level of accomplishment within your business. You must see effectiveness in terms of what I call the **3Vs** - Vision, Values and Voices. Vision offers purposeful direction – i.e. having a destination. Without a vision your employees will end up duplicating their efforts, wasting their energy and therefore becoming inefficient in what they do. Values serve as the guideposts in every organisation, just as societal values inform citizens of a society about what they should see as "right" and "wrong". It means your values will remind your employees of the inherent meaning of their jobs and provide them with guidelines on how they should go about their work. Voice gives employees empowerment and allows them to relate closely with you and other managers in your business, providing essential feedback on changes on the ground. Since realities on the ground change over time, it is important for you and your managers to listen not only to the voices within yourselves but also to those around you. Thus, effectiveness relates to your capability to sense and know the "right things" to do and to guide all your employees to do those "right things" in the right manner. This also means the term effectiveness helps you keep the long term sustainability of your business in mind and always be aware of the dynamics of the environment and adapt accordingly to them.

Any business or organisation may be assessed as having high or low degrees of efficiency and effectiveness. These assessments can be schematically presented in a 2 X 2 matrix as shown in Figure 5.1.The best run businesses are those in which decisions are made to ensure both high levels of effectiveness and efficiency. Such businesses demonstrate excellence in their operational performance as well as strategic management decisions. They will usually have costs under control, employees will be well aware of the tasks they have been delegated to perform, and these will be completed in a timely manner. This means most of the employees will show high levels of commitment and morale, and the long term goals and vision of the organisation will be a source of inspiration and energy for their work.

Figure 5.1 Efficiency and Effectiveness Dimensions of Managerial Decisions

		Effectiveness	
		High	**Low**
Efficiency	**High**	Consistently high performing organisations (demonstrate innovativeness and adaptability)	Organisations characterised by roles, authority structures and routines
	Low	Entrepreneurial and ideologically committed organisations	Consistently low performing organisations (Lacking vision, direction, motivation and skills)

If a business exhibits low levels of efficiency but is highly effective, it might survive, but its cost of operational management and inputs will be suboptimal and this will impact its overall performance. A business with such characteristics may be innovative and capture market shares from competitors, but might do so with high operational costs – barely breaking even or having very little profit. Usually, employee morale in such organisations will be high. But its overall survival will be doubtful. Businesses that are low in effectiveness but high in efficiency tend to focus on immediate tasks and their employees tend to exhibit high work discipline and skills that ensure optimal use of resources. Their short run operational (financial) performances will be high. But their employees will be mostly involved in routine tasks - their creative capacity will remain nearly unexplored.

In a nutshell, you must always aim at raising both their efficiency and effectiveness levels in your business. That is, as a business owner, you must look at both immediate task performance and, at the same time, explore opportunities for long-term growth and sustainability. You must train your employees to focus their attention on efficiency-related decisions, making sure that the tasks at hand are carried out with the minimum possible resources without overstraining their capacities or jeopardizing their job satisfaction.

Implications for Your Business Strategies

To be efficient you must be keenly aware of the limitations of your resources. The saying that "cut your coat according to the size of your cloth" applies here. You must develop a strategy that serves a specific segment of your market and serves your customers well so that they become loyal to your business. This will cut your cost without sacrificing the quality of your services. If you spread your resources too thinly, many of your customers will become dissatisfied and go to your competitors.

Another thing you may need to pay attention to is how efficiently your workers do their work. Waiting time is one measure of efficiency. Make sure that your employees work in real time – e.g.

no one is kept waiting for information from other employees. If you conduct meetings, have a policy that no meeting lasts for more than 45 minutes unless you are discussing something that has long term implications for the business. This requires that you establish a clear purpose and set an objective for each meeting and assess if a meeting is the best way to address the issues that you would want to talk about.

You must also consider using external services for things that other companies can do more efficiently than yourself or employees in your company. For example, instead of employing your own accountant you may consider having some of your accounting functions done by small accounting firms, if their fees are reasonable.

Remember to reward efficiency. If one of your employees figures out how to perform a task in a smart way that will save you money, give him or her an extra vacation day or lunch on the company. It is simple but it raises motivation and increases commitment. Other employees will want to find other smarter ways of helping your business reduce costs.

Managing your business effectively means having a dream. Have a dream of being great in this life. Do not be satisfied with making your first million cedis. Think in dollars and beyond hundred million dollars. It also means that you must keep your focus to achieve your dream. You must not chase every opportunity. Do what you are good at and build knowledge, skills and capabilities to achieve greater things. Never be defeated. Remind yourself that losing a battle does not amount to losing the war.

Chapter Six

Developing and Maintaining Trust with Business Partners

Introduction

Studies of business relations in Ghana show that it is difficult for business people to enter into long term relationships and/or provide credits to each other when doing business. People simply do not trust each other. The lack of trust imposes additional costs on businesses, including shortages of critical inputs, delays in payments of wages and salaries to employees and non-delivery of goods to customers. Ghanaian business-owners therefore generally see the contract enforcement challenges as normal risks of doing business. Research has demonstrated that when business-owners understand and appreciate one another's viewpoints, they are able to arrive at working consensus and manage their relationships more effectively. The trust they build reduces the amount of resources that they spend on monitoring activities of each other. It therefore reduces the cost of operations, and therefore, business performance. It is therefore important for you to develop and maintain trust between your company and your business partners as well as other individuals and institutions that you relate to. This chapter provides you with some guidelines about how to initiate and develop trusting relationships.

Trust as a Foundation of Business

What is trust and how do you create it? David W. Johnson the author of *Reaching Out*, reminds us that trust is a word everyone uses, yet it is a complex concept and difficult to define. In his view, making a choice to trust another person involves the perception that the choice can lead to gains or losses. Whether you will gain or lose in a relationship depends upon the behaviour of the other person. By trusting another person you implicitly believe that the person will act in a manner that will enable you to gain more than you will lose. In other words, people who trust each other believe that their relationships are worth sustaining and therefore actively contribute to their continuity. Thus, trust leads to higher levels of loyalty and long-term collaboration between people. Fukuyama (1995) therefore defines trust as the expectation of regular, honest and co-operative behaviour based on commonly shared norms and values.

Trust between business partners develops and grows through their exchange of experiences. When you engage in information exchange, joint problem solving and mutual learning with your business partners over a period of time your trust in them will grow because both of you will show greater willingness to be flexible in your demands in the face of unanticipated changes. That is, you will be less inclined to take advantage of the difficulties that your partner may run into. In that regard trust complements written contracts between business-owners with the understanding that a contract cannot be expected to address every eventuality and contingency faced in business.

Helpful Hints about Trust

1. Trust is a very complex concept to understand.

2. Trust exists in relationships, not in someone's personality; trust is something that occurs between people, not within people

3. Trust is constantly changing as two people interact

4. Trust is hard to build and easy to destroy

5. The key to building and maintaining trust is being trustworthy; the more accepting and supportive you are of others, the more likely it is that they will come to trust you

6. Trust needs to be appropriate. Never trusting and always trusting are inappropriate.

7. Cooperation increases trust, competition decreases trust

Source: Johnson, David W. (1993) *Reaching Out* 5th Edition (Boston, Allyn and Bacon) p. 67

Note that trust is a risky undertaking in business. For trust to develop between you and your partner, you must be willing to let down your guard (as it is) and become vulnerable to see whether your partner will abuse that vulnerability. This means you will be considered as trusting when you are willing to risk beneficial or harmful outcomes by making yourself vulnerable to other people. Said differently, trust lays the foundation for a mutual confidence among business partners that no party to an exchange will exploit the other's vulnerability. In the management literature, concepts such as honest dealing, openness, acceptance, support and dialogue have been used to describe antecedent conditions for trust building among collaborating business partners.

Trust-building is a learnable skill. Harvy Simkovits (President of Business Wisdom[3]) identifies twelve factors that can help build and sustain trust in a business relationship.

1. **Declaring Intent** - Intent is a fundamental motive people have for doing what they do. When you declare your intent to act in a particular way, you provide your partner with words to measure your actions against. The more you keep your word, the more the overall confidence in your ability to contribute increases. Thus declaring intent up front in any relationship reduces resistance and enhances you and your partner's commitment.

2. **Rapport** - If you can find things in common with another person, this will help you build rapport and help create fertile ground on which to build trust.

3. **Honesty** – This entails always telling the truth about how you see things; offering your true perspective on matters at an opportune time (when the other person is open to your thinking).

---

[3] See http://www.business-wisdom.com/WhoWeAre.html

4. **Sincerity** - This entails demonstrating caring and unconditional positive regard to another person's point of view, even if you disagree with his/her perspective.

5. **Respect for Self and Others** - This entails always talking to and dealing with others as equals and never as if they were lesser than or greater than you; i.e., never criticising them or belittling yourself; saying what you agree with before you say what you disagree with. You demonstrate respect in a relationship when you genuinely take your partner's feedback and viewpoints into account in making your decisions and when you do this on every occasion. Show sensitivity to their interests, wishes and needs. Value them and thank them.

6. **Openness** – This requires fully hearing and understanding the other person's viewpoint; allowing yourself to be impacted by their needs and ideas. Do not punish mistakes. As they can happen, think and speak about them in a result-oriented and forward-looking way. Jointly look with others for solutions and implement actions to avoid that they will happen again.

7. **Competency** – This entails demonstrating your knowledge and know-how around matters of importance to the other person; also demonstrating your ability to get to what is most important to the other person and in being able to differentiate your point of view from theirs. Competence is demonstrated by doing the right thing, in the right way, for the right reasons, in the way that you said you would.

8. **Mutuality** – This requires always working to serve all parties' best interests; not being out just for yourself, or for just one or a few others. If your actions consistently create conditions where every party can win, this will work to bolster everyone's positive regard of you.

9. **Integrity** – This entails walking your talk (having alignment between your words and actions); taking your promises seriously and working sincerely to keep them.

10. **Reliability** – This means being consistent in your behaviour or in your way of being or acting

11. **Admission** - If you make an error, gracefully admit it and explain in a simple way how the error came about.

12. **Recovery** - When you need to break a promise, quickly inform the other person of the bad news, and apologize for not being able to fulfil the promise. You can then make a new promise in order to make it up to your partner.

As indicated above, it is always useful to remember that trust is a risky proposition, and therefore not always appropriate. There are times when it is inadvisable to show high levels of openness and share resources or let down your guard. But if you have a *never trusting mindset* this will make it nearly impossible for you to develop a business relationship that requires some degree of trust to become mutually beneficial.

Chapter Seven

Managing your Employees Well

Introduction

Successful business owners are all aware that the most important resources they have are their employees. The way employees think and act, and the manner in which they interact with other people (colleagues, customers, suppliers, competitors, and government officials etc.) and the relationships that they build through these interactions are all crucial for their own growth and their performance within the business. Their behaviours can improve their companies' chances of achieving their goals or, in some cases, constrain the prospects of achieving them. It is therefore important for you to think carefully about how you select and manage your employees. This chapter discusses issues relating to the selection of your employees, and how you should fire those who hurt your business.

Decisions on Who to Employ

Employment of family members is a normal practice in small one-owner managed businesses in Ghana. You are therefore likely to experience some of the benefits and challenges of employing your relatives. As one of the major breadwinners of the extended family, you are likely to be under immense and persistent pressure to hire family members even when there are no jobs for them. By so doing you will free yourself of the immediate stress your senior brothers, sisters, uncles and aunties are likely to put on you. But this will compromise the growth and viability of your business. Since family members that you employ come easily to the jobs and take their job security for granted, they scarcely feel obliged to improve their skills and do a good job. Non-family members that you employ are likely to adopt the same attitude as the family members in the business. After all, why should they work harder and go the extra mile if the family members do not do so. The net effect is that productivity will be low and business opportunities will go unnoticed because no one, apart from you, is seriously concerned with the survival of the business. In case the business collapses, your relatives may not suffer as you. They will join businesses of other relatives that appear to be doing well or return to subsistence life on the family land.

The questions you should constantly ask yourself are these: Will my business grow if I employ a specific family member? How can I avoid the family pressure without losing face within the family?

> *The best executive is the one who has sense enough to pick good men to do what he wants done, and self-restraint enough to keep from meddling with them while they do it.*
>
> — *Theodore Roosevelt*

Some successful business owners that I have interviewed over the years have found creative solutions to the family pressure. They simply withdraw themselves from the extended family during the formative years of their businesses. That is, they deliberately decide not to participate in most social and ceremonial functions of their families in order to avoid the predatory demands of the families during periods where cash flows in the businesses are limited and every single cedi or penny is required to grow the business. They also cleverly avoid employing family members by assigning the personnel functions in their businesses either to a foreign employee or someone outside their ethnic groups. These non-family managers have been able to adhere to the formal rules of employment (e.g. insistence on good qualifications and skills) and have disregarded family connections in the assessment of the qualifications of job applicants. When they have built substantial financial resources and are confident that family claims cannot jeopardise their organic growth ambitions, they re-join the family and participate fully in the social activities to which they are invited. The family then welcomes them with joy, just like the biblical prodigal son. But not all business-owners have the moral courage to adopt this approach. You must work out an arrangement that you consider appropriate for you.

Employing Talented Workers

It is important to find workers that have the skills you need to address immediate problems in your business and keep the current business activities going. But it is equally important to look ahead – i.e. into the future. You must therefore employ talented workers – i.e. those who are creative enough to spot new opportunities and are willing to learn and grow with the business. Talented workers do not only find innovative solutions to business problems you may face. They are also active in creating new client relationships.

To start with, you must train yourself in identifying young and talented people and understand the context in which their talents can flourish. You must then provide them with the proper investment, guidance and opportunities for them to grow. There are several ways you can go about this. One approach is to establish a sound performance appraisal system, which not only evaluates a person's performance, but also identifies promotion potential.

Once you have identified your talented employees, you need to establish an effective method of developing and promoting them. Managing these people requires focus, resources and commitment. For example, you must encourage them to participate in setting the goals in their units or departments. This will give them greater motivation. But progress in achieving these goals must be monitored. If the goals are achieved more quickly than expected, or if they have found more efficient solutions to problems they face in the process, you must remember to reward them.

Make a conscious effort to learn about the passions of each them. It is often said that if a person is very passionate about what he or she is doing it becomes extremely difficult to give up in the face of difficulties. Others working with the passionate person can tap into this passionate energy as well. Therefore, if you are aware of what your talented employees are passionate about, this will enable you to allocate responsibilities in the way that strengthens their commitment.

Firing Employees that Hurt Your Business

Firing employees can be a difficult decision for some of you. The main challenge for many small business owners is how to break the news firmly but gently, particularly when you have worked closely with the employee for some years or if the employee is a family member. This is understandable – it is an integral part of being a human being. We simply do not want to hear bad news or confront a bad situation squarely and find a solution.

But hanging onto the wrong people is not evidence of good business management. You may need to let some people go in order to help your business grow. But give them sufficient opportunity to redeem themselves before making the final decision. You therefore need to discuss your concerns about the individual's poor performance with him or her. Find out if the problem is really the worker or the work environment and if more training or guidance will help. Remember that employee incompetence may be the direct result of your own management failure. But, as we noted earlier, family employees hardly demonstrate the drive to work diligently under the leadership of a family member in order to build a viable enterprise.

Here are some tips you may follow to make it a bit easier for you:

1. Provide each employee with written job descriptions that outline the minimum required for them to do. Discuss the job description with them and make sure that the contents are not misunderstood

2. Do periodic evaluations of the employee's performance and discuss the assessment with them. Agree on what must be done for them to improve performance if you find their performance below expectation.

3. Inform them clearly that the consequences of continuous poor performance will be firing.

4.   Avoid the following mistakes when you are firing an employee:

   a.   **Don't talk about yourself:** If you say, "I know how you feel," or "I don't want to do this," you seem more worried about yourself than about the employee.

   b.   **Don't sugar-coat:** Don't offer false praise and tell them all the reasons why you think they are great. It clouds the issue and can be confusing.

   c.   **Stay calm and avoid being emotional** - Stick to the purpose of this meeting factually. Present the case to the employee as a necessary decision for the company and the employee.

Chapter Eight

Choose an Appropriate Leadership Style

Introduction

Successful entrepreneurs will tell you that you cannot achieve sustainable growth by bullying your employees. If you do so, you may be successful for a short while. But your business may easily run into trouble because you have not provided your employees with a growth-oriented leadership. Thus, your choice of leadership style is important for your performance. The importance of leadership for growth is also reflected in Johann Wolfgang Von Goethe's statement that "a great person attracts great people and knows how to hold them together". Thus, leadership can be seen as the process of giving meaningful direction. That is, the direction provided by leaders must be seen by followers to be meaningful in terms of their own goals and ambitions in life.

Reading this chapter will help you gain insight into the types of leadership styles that will encourage employees to go the extra mile to help you achieve the business goals that you set. You will also note that employees' perception of your leadership style will determine how they behave at work while you are there and when you are away. They base this perception on inferences and observations of your past behaviours when they see you in action or what other employees say to them about you. This defines the psychological contract they have with you.

Task versus Employee-Oriented Leadership Styles

Management scholars classify leadership styles into two broad categories: (1) task-oriented leadership style, and (2) employee-oriented style. A task-oriented leader is more concerned with getting the job done than seeking his subordinates' growth and personal satisfaction. They therefore supervise their subordinates very closely. Such leaders also believe that their employees will be motivated when they have clear-cut goals and know the rewards and punishments they will receive if they fulfil their tasks or fail to do so.

The employee-oriented leaders, on the other hand, tend to encourage friendly, trusting and mutually respectful relationship with their subordinates. They are also seen as being powerful and having wide range of reach. Being powerful does not mean being despotic. It rather means using soft power to create a working environment that makes your employees highly satisfied with their jobs. Studies have also shown a positive link between employee's job satisfaction and their desire to align their personal goals with those of the companies in which they work and a feeling of obligation to continue to work for the company.

The two styles of leadership can be practised by the same persons, depending on the leadership situations in which they find themselves or the maturity and competences of the employees in which they are in charge. I use the term "maturity" here to mean the willingness and ability of a person to take responsibility for directing his or her own behaviour. In this sense, a mature subordinate is one who demonstrates a strong desire for achievement and willingness to accept responsibility. It means you may adopt a task-oriented leadership style in handling employees that you have newly appointed. But as they become more mature, it is more appropriate for you to become more supportive than instructive, giving them a free hand to handle tasks assigned them. You must, therefore, constantly assess the level of motivation, ability and task knowledge of your employees to determine which leadership style combination can be successfully employed. It also means that you must treat your employees as individuals and choose your leadership styles to fit the requirements of each of them.

Siong Guan Lim and Joanne H. Lim in their book *The Leader, The Teacher & You,* explain it this way, "if a leader sees his role as not just to lead well for today but to build well for the future, his best contribution then is as a teacher: identifying potential, recognizing effort, encouraging ideas, and pursuing excellence with a continuous drive for the organisation to be the best it can be and the people to be the best they can be" p. 251

> *The challenge of leadership is to be strong, but not rude; be kind, but not weak; be bold, but not bully; be thoughtful, but not lazy; be humble, but not timid; be proud, but not arrogant; have humor, but without folly.*
>
> —*Jim Rohn*

Empowerment: Giving Your Employees a Sense of Ownership

The success of your business will depend very much on what your employees do when you turn your back. Do they take their tasks seriously and exhibit a sense of responsibility to make things happen the way you would want them to happen? Researchers have found out that the extent to which employees are committed to their work depends on the sense of ownership they feel. Ownership in this regard is a psychological factor and not a financial ownership. Your employees are aware that you are the owner of the business and the only financial reward they get is what you give them. But if you forge a positive relationship with them and make them share the organisation's vision, they will make this vision part of their own value systems and put the achievement of these goals before their own self-interest. They will find meaning and satisfaction in working for you and will therefore protect your interest even when you are away. This requires that you exhibit enthusiasm and optimism and also communicate clear and realistic expectations in your interactions with them.

The dominant management practice in Ghana is that employees are required to strictly follow instructions, rather than to think and find solutions to work-related problems that they face. They are expected to be thankful for the security which their employers offer them in wages and benefits. Avoid this leadership style. Be bold enough to tell your employees: "You are in control, solve problems you encounter in the best manner possible". Research has also shown that involving people early on during problem finding permits them to exercise their full creative potential. By transferring ownership of problems, you will facilitate change in the mindset of your employees rather than impose it.

Mentoring Your Key Employees

You need a strategy to do that. A key element in any such strategy is to have an active programme for personal growth and career development. This requires providing on-going training, and, especially, the chance to be mentored. Studies have shown that employees that are mentored stay on the job longer than those that are left to sink or swim. If employees do not know what is expected of them or how they should go about their tasks, they feel frustrated and leave the company at the next available opportunity. Those who remain are those who do not have any real options. I guess you would want your employees to remain with you, not simply because they do not have anywhere else to go. Management is not about a manager decreeing what should occur and followers responding in a mechanical way. Frequent advice given to business-owners and managers is that they should act as mentors and cheerleaders. That means they should adopt a hands-on approach in guiding new employees. As they gain and display more creative skills in their work processes, managers must change their style of leadership from a coaching role to being more facilitative. Cheerleading means that as a business-owner, you must act in a manner that makes your employees feel good about themselves – i.e. spread joy.

The management literature identifies seven main roles a mentor can assume. But the appropriate role would depend on the needs of the specific employees of the company. Each of the seven roles is described below.

Teacher: As a teacher, a mentor needs to teach the mentee the skills and knowledge required to perform his/her position successfully.

This role requires the mentor to have the required skills and knowledge. He must also have a rich pool of experience that would enable him to share the wisdom of past mistakes. Thus the richer and more varied the mentor's experience the better.

Guide: As a guide, the mentor helps the employees navigate through the inner workings of the organisation and make sense of the unwritten rules within the company. The inner workings of the organisation are simply the "behind the scenes" dynamics, or office politics, that are not always apparent, but are crucial to know. The "unwritten rules" can include the special procedures an office follows, the guidelines that are not always documented and policies under consideration.

Counsellor: The role of counsellor requires the mentor to establish a lasting and open relationship. In order to create a trusting relationship, the mentor needs to stress confidentiality and show respect for the employees that confide in him – e.g. by not disclosing personal information that employees share with him.

Motivator: Motivation is an inner drive that compels a person to succeed. Through encouragement, support and incentives, mentors can motivate employees to succeed. One of the most effective ways to encourage an employee is to provide frequent, positive feedback during assigned tasks. Positive feedback is a great "morale booster." It removes doubt and builds self-esteem that result in a sense of accomplishment.

Sponsor: A sponsor creates opportunities for employees. These opportunities can relate directly to the job or indirectly to the overall professional development of individual employees. The goal of the mentor is to provide as much exposure for the employee as possible, with a minimum of risk. Opportunities should challenge and instruct without destroying an employee's self-esteem.

Coach: Coaching is a complex and extensive process, and is not always an easy skill to perform. Specifically, coaching involves feedback. A mentor needs to give different kinds of feedback as the situation demands: positive feedback to reinforce behaviour and constructive feedback to change behaviour. Both types of feedback are critical to the professional growth of the mentee. Feedback should be frequent, specific, and based on direct observation of the mentee (not second-hand information).

Advisor: This role requires the mentor to help the mentee develop professional interests and set realistic career goals. The mentor needs to think about where the mentee wants to go professionally and help set career goals. Career goals should be specific, time-framed, results-oriented, relevant, reachable and flexible to accommodate the changing dynamics of the organisation.

> *A leader takes people where they want to go. A great leader takes people where they don't necessarily want to go, but ought to be.*
>
> *—Rosalynn Carter*

The ACHIEVE Model

Hersey and Goldsmith[4] identified seven variables regarding to effective performance management: ability, understanding, organisational support, motivation, performance feedback, validity and environment. They describe these variables in their "ACHIEVE" – model. It consists of the following:

1. **Ability:** This refers to the employee's knowledge, experience and skills, which are the abilities to complete the specific task

---

[4] See Hersey, Paul (2007). *Management of Organizational behavior*, Ninth edition, Upper Saddle River, p.72

66

successfully. As noted earlier, strengthening employees' ability entails providing them with task-relevant education and facilitating their acquisition of task-relevant experience and task-relevant skill.

2. **Clarity:** This refers to an understanding and acceptance of what to do, when to do it, and how to do it. Employees must know clearly what the major goals and objectives are, how they should be accomplished and their priority. Employees should be encouraged to raise questions for further clarification on things they are not sure about.

3. **Help:** You must always make sure that your employees have all the help they need to accomplish an assigned task. This may include issues such as adequate budget, suitable equipment and facilities.

4. **Incentive**: You must always remember that not all people could be equally motivated to accomplish all tasks. External incentives are always useful.

- **Evaluation**: An evaluation system includes day-to-day performance feedback and informal and formal periodic reviews. A good evaluation system can make employees clear about their performance and to improve the performance further.

- **Validity**: Your decisions must always be tested against the existing laws and moral codex of the country. This will provide you with legitimacy within your industry and make your employees proud to be working in your company.

- **Environment**: Always keep changes with the external operational environment in mind when you make strategic decisions.

Box 8-1
The Personality of a Good Leader

1. Learn to be strong, but not rude. Some people mistake rudeness for strength. Do not be that type of leader

2. Learn to be kind but not weak. Kindness must not be mistaken for weakness. Kindness is a certain type of strength. For example, you must be kind enough to tell your employees the truth about their performance and what they can do to improve it.

3. Learn to be bold, but not a bully. To build your influence, you've got to be willing to take the first arrow, tackle the first problem, and discover the first sign of trouble.

4. Learn to be humble, but not timid. Do not mistake timidity for humility.

5. Learn to be proud, but not arrogant. The worst kind of arrogance is arrogance from ignorance. It's when you don't know that you don't know.

6. Learn to accept the fact that not everyone will like you

Some scholars argue that a good leader's true identity is revealed when he leads from within. This means that the leader is able to implant his values in the inner core of his followers' life and is able to generate capability, capacity, confidence and the zeal to accomplish feats beyond the remotest fantasies of the leader. This means every individual follower lives his own and to bring their own dreams to bear on their actions, using the fundamental values of his mentor as a platform. In this way the leader achieves continuity and change in the lives of his followers. I believe that this advice is appropriate for a business owner as well.

Chapter Nine

Communicate with Maturity

Introduction

It is often said that clear communication is the most important key to a business manager's success. Open and effective communication facilitates the day-to-day operations within a business, ensuring that everything runs smoothly and reduces waste of time on unessential issues. So to grow as a manager, you must learn how to be an effective and compelling communicator. And if you want your company to succeed, you and your team have to master the art of clear communication together, as well. By using these and other strategies, you and your employees can reach new levels of excellence.

But Ghanaian managers are very often accused by their employees of not communicating clearly enough regarding roles, goals, expectations and the importance of specific behaviours for achieving their goals. Some actually "over-communicate" (i.e. communicate inappropriately through outbursts, anger or blaming). They also often fail to communicate their vision in a way that is meaningful.

The challenge you face as a business owner and manager is to learn how to communicate with maturity. That is, how can you be sure that you are communicating with thoughtfulness and the knowledge that inspire your employees to exert themselves in their work and exceed your expectations? Your maturity reflects your ability to manage your emotions, to assess the emotional state of others and to influence their behaviour. Thus, communicating with maturity will result in fewer disagreements and less drama in your relationships with your employees, but also with government officials and business associates.

This chapter provides you with some general observations of the requirements of good communication and some tips about how you can improve your ability to communicate.

The Nature of Communication

The word communication comes from the Latin word "communis", meaning "to share or to participate". Thus, communication involves the effort of people to get in touch with one another and to make them understood. In business, it is often said that about 75% of the manager's time is spent on communicating business decisions to others, including strategies targets, and rules, policies. But effective communication is not a one-way transmission; it is a dialogue. That is when information is shared accurately between two or more people with receivers responding with the view of seeking clarity or sharing other types of information that enriches the pool of knowledge available to the participants in the communication process. Successful communications also tend to strengthen the feeling of togetherness between the participants in the communication. Communication is therefore a social activity.

It will be a good idea to learn to adapt your communication style to the persons you are interacting with or to the situations you find yourself in. Your goal must be to encourage the people you communicate with to react to meet the goals of the communication. When you communicate you must be aware that the target audience may be either within your company or outside. The location of your target audience may influence the purpose of your communication. Your internal communication may have one or a combination of the following objectives:

1. Bind your employees together and improve morale in your business.
2. Facilitate planning and co-ordination of your business activities.
3. Help your employees make the right decisions.

Your external communication may be directed at employees in other businesses and organisations that you relate to as well as your customers. You would want to persuade them to behave in a way that helps you achieve your business goals. Whoever you communicate with, it pays to see the person as if he or she is a king or a queen. Treat the person with respect and dignity, and you will nearly always get a positive response from the individual. This is a golden rule in communication. This is what some people refer to as communicating with maturity. The understanding is that because maturity affects emotional control and reasoning, it affects individual's ability to work together and to successfully make joint decisions.

When speaking, you should consider whether you would want your employees to speak in the same way to the same audience. If not, you must adjust your communication style. Remember that your employees will tend to emulate how they see you act and communicate. If your employees see you using an active listening style and empathetic tone with customers, they are more likely to do the same. When you are open to the ideas of others and often praise, your employees will tend to follow suit.

Practise Active Listening

An important aspect of communication is the ability to listen. Active listening should always be your goal. Try to focus on both the verbal and nonverbal language of people you interact with. Active listening involves concentrating only on the speaker and ignoring outside interruptions. Active listeners also refrain from interrupting, give the speaker time to finish, show they are listening by doing things like nodding or smiling.

Listening is particularly crucial when emotions are high. This could be in situations when employees or customers interact with you in a state of anger, resentment and excitement. Generally, people feel acknowledged when others validate their feelings. If you ignore the feelings of those you relate, to you can create distance between yourself and the people, and this may negatively affect the working environment in your company.

71

Listening is also particularly important when employees are sharing ideas. When managers stop listening to ideas, employees stop offering them. That means managers are essentially cut off from the creativity and expertise of their employees.

It is therefore advisable to spend a little bit of time each day learning, reading and practising essential communication techniques. It may seem difficult to become an excellent communicator, but with practice you'll soon discover that you can do it.

Your Ego and Your Communication Style

Your style of communication will also affect the degree of motivation and commitment of your employees to their duties. Your preferred style of communication may be an attribute of your personality. Berne's (1964) Transaction Analysis (TA) theory provides a useful frame of reference for understanding the role of personality in interpersonal communication processes. He argues that individuals' personality can be seen in their manifestation of three ego states: (1) child ego-state, (2) parent ego-state, and (3) adult ego state. These ego states represent consistent patterns of feeling, thinking and experience and do not relate to age or family status.

The "child ego state" is a metaphor that describes behaviours originating from impulses, i.e. unpredictable emotional outbursts that are normally associated with children. Individuals whose dominant behaviours are conditioned by their child ego state are likely to change abruptly from manifesting hatred for an individual to love, depending on the situation and their temperament at a given time. Their non-verbal expression may include scowl, frown, grumbling, shouting, giggling.

If your behaviours derive mainly from the "parent ego state", you are most likely to be judgmental and critical in your interpersonal communication settings. You are also likely to use such words as "should" and "ought to" in your oral communication when referring to the behaviour of other people. You may also be likely to be frequently seen shaking your head, patting people of their shoulder, or pointing a finger accusingly. In other words, you will tend to put yourself in the parent position when dealing with other people. Such an orientation is unlikely to create a good atmosphere for interpersonal communication, particularly if the people you are communicating with are sensitive about their status and positions and expect to be treated with utmost respect.

The "adult ego state" is characterised by encouraging people to be less hasty in their conclusions and willing to seek information and knowledge about various issues with which they are involved before making decisions. If you communicate from an "adult ego state", you are likely to be more patient and restrictive in your choice of words and emotional expressions. You will frequently use such expressions as "is that right", "is it okay to do?"..."What would you say to this suggestion?"

As individuals, we are likely to demonstrate any of these ego states, and often shift unknowingly from one to the other. For instance, in front of our boss, we may exhibit a child ego-state, whereas towards our subordinates, we will exhibit parent ego-state or adult ego-state. All three ego states add value to our lives; however, when one of them disturbs the equilibrium, an analysis and reconfiguration are desired. We all find ourselves in situations where we may think that we can elicit a response from someone, or if we can get them to do what we want, then this can make us feel that we are in control. But this may make the people we interact with a bit insecure. This insecurity might trigger resentment. But if you instead respond to others by appreciating and listening to them, using respectful tones, perceiving the facts, considering alternatives, having a long-term view of the suggestions they make, you are behaving as an adult and they will respond from their adult ego state.

The Story of the Blind Beggar

This story is told by Song Guan Lim and Joanne H. Lim in their book *The Leader, The Teacher & You*. It illustrates the power of communication in changing human behaviour. Reflect on it.

> A blind boy sat on the steps of a building with a hat by his feet. He held up a sign that said "I am blind, please help me". There were only a few coins in the hat. A man walking by took a few coins from his pocket and dropped them into the hat. He then took the sign, turned it around, and wrote several words. He put the sign back so that everyone who walked by could see it.
>
> Soon, the hat began to fill up. A lot more people were giving money to the blind boy.
>
> That afternoon, the man who had changed the sign came to see how things were. The boy recognised his footsteps and asked. "Were you the one who changed my sign this morning? What did you write?"
>
> The man said, "I only wrote the truth. I said what you said but in a different way."
>
> What he had written was: "Today is a beautiful day and I cannot see it."

What made the difference?

The first sign simply asked for help. But the second sign reminded all those who passed by and could see how privileged they were to see and enjoy the beautiful day.

An important lesson to learn from this story is this: "Think differently. There is always a better way to communicate. The manner you communicate to others determines the response you get from them".

Chapter Ten

Engage in Fast Learning

Introduction

It is generally acknowledged in management literature that knowledge is an important source of competitive advantage. This requires learning. Learning is a process of acquiring and sharing information, as well as reflecting on the information acquired. This process must be grounded in the actions of everyday situations. Knowledge acquired in a given situation can be and are transferred to similar situations. Knowledge management scholars inform that social processes influence the way we think, perceive, solve problems, and share knowledge with others. We frequently learn by making mistakes. In business, just as in other fields of life, learning from others is one of the key mechanisms to generate new knowledge. You must learn to tap into the stock of knowledge of your employees and business partners. This chapter provides you with some guidelines on how to learn.

Learning and Absorptive Capacity

Absorptive capacity is the term management scholars use to describe the ability people have to understand the knowledge received from others.

It is often said that when people *do* want to learn something new, they tend to assess their ability to absorb the new knowledge and match this against the outcomes of applying the new knowledge. But very often our assessments of ourselves (i.e. what we know and don't know, skills we have and don't have) can be inaccurate. We frequently think that we know a lot more about running our business than we actually do. We are therefore not prepared to invest time and resources to upgrade our knowledge in any specific way. This self-deception surely diminishes any appetite for development. This blocks our mind and reduces our absorptive capacity.

There is another factor that reduces our desire to learn. This is the tendency we all have of keeping within our comfort zones. Once we become good or even excellent at some things, we rarely want to go back to being *not* good at other things. But the first step to learning something new is to accept the inadequacy of one's existing pool of knowledge. So to learn fast you must accept that your knowledge in some aspects of running your business can be improved. Do not feel embarrassed by this; rather accept it as the best opportunity you have to grow your business.

Four Stages of Learning/Hierarchy of Competence

The learning literature identifies four stages of learning – or what some scholars call the hierarchy of competence. This learning model suggests that individuals are initially unaware of how little they know, or unconscious of their incompetence. As they recognise their incompetence, they consciously acquire a skill, they then consciously use it. Eventually, the skill can be utilised without it being consciously thought through: the individual is then said to have acquired unconscious competences. These are explained briefly below.

1. **Unconscious incompetence**

    This is a situation when you are doing something wrong and you do not know you are doing it in a wrong way. This means you do not know that you do not have the skills and competences required to accomplish the task. At its best this can be described as 'blissful ignorance' and in rare cases is a great enabler of innovation, as it allows people to attain results that normal ways of thinking may prevent them from achieving. However, generally this is not the case and 'not knowing what you don't know' is a real disabler of advancement.

76

2.   **Conscious incompetence**
Though the individual does not understand or know how to do something, he or she does recognise the deficit, as well as the value of a new skill in addressing the deficit. The making of mistakes can be integral to the learning process at this stage.

3.   **Conscious competence**
The individual understands or knows how to do something. However, demonstrating the skill or knowledge requires concentration. It may be broken down into steps, and there is heavy conscious involvement in executing the new skill.

4.   **Unconscious competence**
The individual has had so much practice with a skill that it has become "second nature" and can be performed easily. As a result, the skill can be performed while executing another task. The individual may be able to teach it to others, depending upon how and when it was learned.

This model helps you understand the emotions you will experience during the learning process and helps you manage your expectations of success, so that you don't try to achieve too much, too soon. It will also help you stay motivated when times get tough when learning new skills. It is also useful in coaching and training situations, because it allows you to be in touch with what your employees are thinking and feeling. You can then help them understand their emotions as they learn new skills and encourage them when they are feeling disillusioned.

Learning in the Community of Your Employees

Management scholars also say that companies learn through their employees and most of the learning takes place in specific work situations where employees interact. But to learn we first need to *unlearn* some of the knowledge we already have. Unlearning is a process through which we discard obsolete and misleading knowledge, replacing them with new knowledge.

When you see that you can do better than you are actually doing, you are usually motivated to find out what you are doing wrongly and what you can do to correct your errors. Correcting errors provides a learning experience that ensures that similar problems can be effectively addressed in the future. But just correcting errors will not enable you to do something extraordinarily or improve your performance in comparison to your immediate competitors. You must instead continuously ask the following question: "what has prevented me and my company from questioning practices that have resulted in the errors in the first place"? This will help you take a serious (somewhat painful) look at your habits in the company to help you change your mindset and help your employees change theirs as well. With a new mindset you will do things differently and improve your fortune.

Chapter Eleven

Generating and Sustaining Positive Human Energy

Introduction

There is also what some call emotional knowledge. For example, business leaders are encouraged to find ways to energise themselves and their workers, to recoil to rooms of silence and to engage in meditation and self-reflection in order to sharpen their intuitive capabilities to make decisions that could change the fortune of their companies. Those who accept and apply the concept of emotional knowledge maintain that human energy is most effectively used when it supplements, not supplants, rational decision-making techniques. These scholars draw distinction between negative and positive energies that derive from some specific human attributes. The negative attributes include greed, selfishness, manipulation, secrecy, distrust, anxiety, self-absorption, fear, burnout, and feelings of abuse that tend to derail organisational efforts. Positive attributes include appreciation, collaboration, virtuousness, vitality, and meaningfulness. Employees in such businesses are characterised by trustworthiness, resilience, wisdom and humility. This chapter provides you with some insight into this line of thinking.

Characteristics of Human Energy at the Workplace

It is often argued that when employees are managed as "resources" they tend to do what other resources do: they become depleted or absent – they burn out or move to another company. If this happens to your company, it will result in substantial investment losses (including knowledge leakages). The concept of "human assets" has, therefore, been introduced into the literature to emphasise the inherent positive characteristics of employees. Managed as "assets" employees are expected to flourish and grow in value. The concept of human energy or fundamental life condition is another concept that has recently entered into the management literature. This concept takes us beyond *who* we are as humans as reflected in our rational being and belief systems and gets us closer to an understanding of that aspect of our being that makes us uniquely and typically human. Religious scholars describe this aspect of human life as the human spirit or soul.

In physics, energy is the ability or capacity to do work or to produce change. It is common for energy to be converted from one form to another. However, the law of conservation of energy (a fundamental law of physics) states that although energy can be changed in form, it can neither be created nor destroyed. Therefore, understanding psychic energy is not only a matter of assessing the conditions of the energy as such, but also the circumstances that determine, inhibit, and generate certain conditions of energy. It also requires an understanding of the consequences of particular energy conditions and the kind of transformation processes that energy can potentially undergo in order to produce change.

Energy generally exists in a *latent* form and is - as such - not visible to people. That is, human beings are not aware of their energy until some external causes trigger it into a *manifest* form. Latent energy turns into manifest energy within organisations through interaction. As people interact, they experience the flow of energy within and between each other. The flow may be experienced as more or less intensive and over short or long periods of time. But the interaction also produces transformation within and between people who interact. In other words, there is a simultaneous process of transformation and manifestation of energy occurring through interaction processes among employees. It is this simultaneity of transformation and manifestation that produces differences in the dynamic capabilities of businesses.

Think for a moment about how you felt during the latest business meeting you attended and think about how the people at the meeting behaved. This will help you get a picture of how human energy manifests itself in practice. In situations where the energy in which the meeting is embedded is marked by strength and intensity, all the participants tend to be well prepared and focused. Everybody contributes to the discussions with openness and joy. Important decisions are made swiftly based on thorough and swift dialogue. But if the strength of the energy is low, most of the participants will appear to be less prepared and key persons may be absent from the meeting. Many participants may feel disorganised and frustrated, doing all other things than focusing on the central points of discussion – e.g. glancing through other papers, checking mails, leaving to get some more coffee, etc.

Energy Transmitters and Human Life Tendencies

We have noted earlier that individuals are transmitters of energy within organisations. The transmission takes place during interpersonal relations and/or group interactions. Here language and emotions combine to transmit the latent energy inherent within the individuals to one another. A typical situation in which energy transmission occurs within organisations is during interactions between personnel at different levels of organisational hierarchy. The transmission process is often self-reinforcing. That is, positive energy manifestation sets off a spiral of positive energies, while an initial negative energy manifestation produces the reverse effect.

Whether or not an individual's behaviour manifests an invigorating (positive) or weakening (negative) energy in an organisation or a group will depend on four sets of factors: (1) the *basic life tendencies* of the individual; (2) the events in his/her *life history;* (3) the *manifested collective energy* within the ambient environment (e.g. organisation); and (4) the *socialisation process* or culture that has shaped his/her life. The diversity of individual life tendencies provides each organisation with unique potentials for transmission of energy. It is this feature that defines the degree of organisational agility, as well as the non-immutability and non-substitutability of organisational resources. That is, the ability of one organisation to exhibit superior competitive capabilities over other organisations within a given industry and to manage linkages (local

81

and international) may be understood through the psychic energy construct.

Individual life tendencies are shaped by events from history. Each individual's journey through life is laced with challenges from birth to death. During this span of life, the cumulative experiences (i.e. ways in which individuals tackle the complex set of events in their lives) provide the foundations of their basic life tendencies. Asian religious scholars suggest that some of these events may pre-date birth itself. They are also shaped by socialisation and upbringing, i.e. the culture of the societies within which a particular individual has been raised. This is combined (at work) with the patterns of socialisation and the rules of accepted behaviour that have guided the individual's life experience. Psychologists attempt to understand these basic tendencies as the individual's personality.

Borrowing again from Asian religious philosophies, we can analytically classify the fundamental life tendencies of human beings into ten hierarchically ordered categories: these are Hell, Hunger, Animality, Anger, Tranquillity, Rapture, Learning, Realization, Altruism and Wisdom/Compassion. The quality and value of the energy manifested through each life condition is different. Each life condition is thus considered to have its own type of catalytic potential. Technically speaking, the states of life condition are the fields through which the energies flow, not the psychic energies themselves. They are like doors which may be unlocked by certain conditions and circumstances. The ten life conditions can be divided in two broad groups, the lower level life conditions and the higher level life conditions, as explained below.

The Lower Level Life Conditions

The first six states are called the *six lower level life conditions*. These are hell, hunger, animality, anger, tranquillity and rapture. They have in common the fact that their emergence or disappearance is governed by external circumstances. Take the example of a firm with a strong desire to find someone to invest in a new risky idea. That desire reflects an organisational life condition akin to "hunger". If a manager finds an investor, especially after a long search, a feeling of ecstasy and fulfilment ensues (i.e. they find themselves in the state of rapture). By and by, potential rivals with similar ideas appear on the scene, and the managers become jealous (i.e. in the state of anger). The manifestation of the anger may drive the venture partner away. Crushed by despair (i.e. in the state of hell), the managers are filled with frustration. In this way, many of us – individually as well as collectively (in organisations) – spend time shuttling back and forth among the six lower level life conditions without ever realising that we are being controlled by our reactions to the environment.

The Higher Level Life Conditions

The next two states – *learning* and *realisation* – come about when top management of an organisation recognise that everything experienced in the six lower life conditions of the organisational life is impermanent, and they begin to seek some enduring or higher level vision that can drive its organisational life and development. These two states plus the next two – *altruism* and *compassion/wisdom* – may be called higher life tendencies. Unlike the six lower tendencies, which are passive reactions to the environment, these four higher tendencies are achieved through deliberate effort – i.e. proactive strategic orientation based on ethical probity. Organisations whose manifest collective energies are guided by the four higher life conditions are no longer prisoners to their own reactions.

Building Positive Human Energy

As a business manager, you will notice that one of the greatest challenges you face in your management process is the distraction of the mind. While your efforts are focused on getting one job done your mind keeps on reminding you of the many other things that need to be done. Your employees face similar problems. This reduces the overall positive energy that you all devote to accomplishing important tasks and becoming productive in your business. You need to nurture the energy base of the organisation through positive

83

interactions. Some people call this "relational energy" management.

Interactions are energising in several ways. If you, as the owner of the business, show genuine love for your job and are fully present and attentive when you interact with your employees and demonstrate a general happy attitude to your work, you will energise many of your employees. You will give them hope even in situations when things may not seem to be moving in the right direction. In this regard, you will become an important source of relational energy at the workplace. The more people you energise, the higher your work performance. This occurs because people want to be around you. You attract talent, and people are more likely to devote their discretionary time to your projects. This is one reason why some businesses succeed while others fail within the same environment.

Chapter Twelve

Managing Your Time Effectively

Introduction

Since we all have only 24 hours a day, the manner in which we use every minute of the day is important to our success as individuals and as business owners and managers. You know from experience that it is just as ineffective to waste time on things that are not urgent as it is to waste it on things that are not important. This chapter provides you some illustrative examples that can help you organise your time effectively and help your employees do the same. If you take the guidelines here seriously and put them into effect, you will develop a new business culture that will raise your productivity and performance without any extra effort or resources.

The Key to Effective Time Management

The word "urgent" is a decisive term in time management. Any task you label "urgent" will attract your immediate attention - no matter how trivial it may be. It acts as a tyrant – urging you unceasingly to pay attention to it. If you don't, you will go through the rest of the day or week with a sense of guilt. If you are that type of manager, you are in a perpetual psychological trouble. It is therefore important for you to decide which activities merit the label "urgent". This is the first step in taking control over how you spend your time.

Another key word in time management is "important". If you label a task important, you must devote a substantial proportion of your time to it. You can only find enough time to the important tasks if you remove "urgent" labels that you have attached to unimportant tasks. The time saved then makes it possible for you to attach urgent labels to important tasks that are being neglected.

The wisdom you can derive from this simple principle is illustrated in Figure 12.1

Figure 12.1: A Framework for Time Allocation

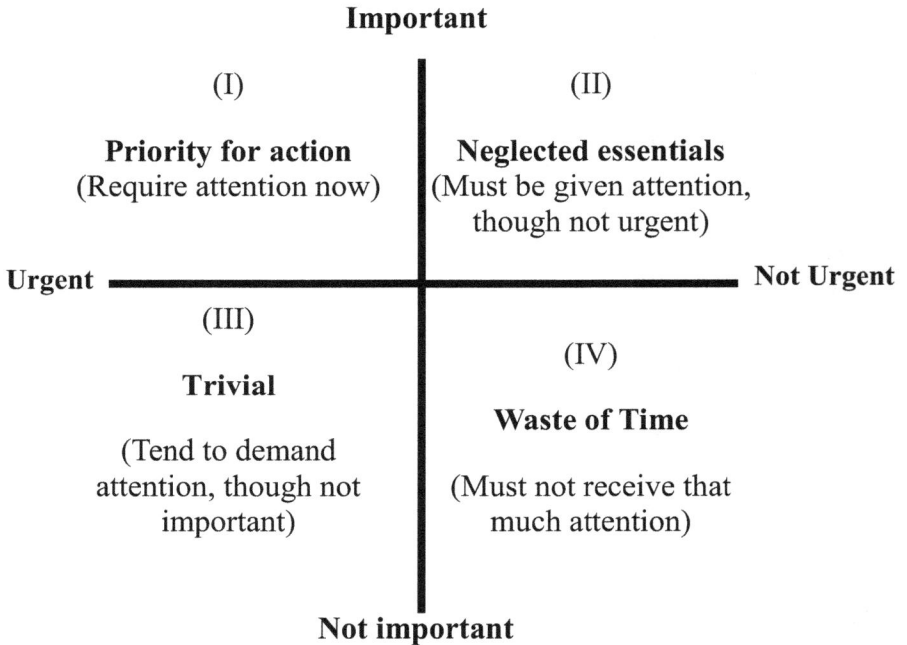

Important

(I)	(II)
Priority for action	**Neglected essentials**
(Require attention now)	(Must be given attention, though not urgent)

Urgent ———————————————— **Not Urgent**

(III)	(IV)
Trivial	**Waste of Time**
(Tend to demand attention, though not important)	(Must not receive that much attention)

Not important

It is obvious that you must devote time to tasks that you place in quadrant I - doing things that are both important and urgent. Conversely, as little time as possible should be spent in quadrant IV - on things that are neither important nor urgent.

There is a tension between the other two quadrants. On the one hand, urgent things demand attention - even when they are not important (quadrant III). On the other hand, important things - even when they appear not to be urgent (quadrant II) - ought to get done. Since the urgent label is always compelling, you are likely to put important tasks on one side, while time is absorbed with the unimportant.

Think about how much time you spend entertaining visitors (friends and family members) that walk into your office without any prior invitation. Our social norms label such visits "urgent", although not important in the light of your business obligations. How do you deal with such visits? Are you bold enough to tell the visitors that you will not have time for them? This is a major challenge that Ghanaian managers face. The way you deal with your visitors will guide your employees as to how they should treat similar visitors and help correct the ineffective use of time in your business.

If you accept the view that you will inevitably spend time on things that you label "urgent", my advice to you is to label things you want done "urgent" and remove the label "urgent" from all the things on which you do not want to waste time. In this way, you will not have any guilty feeling in paying attention to the urgent tasks, since everything that is labelled urgent is now also important. Thus, paying attention to the urgent means that all one's time is spent in the priority area on things that are both urgent and important. Getting focused means raising the urgency on important things that have been pushed to the bottom of the pile. To get neglected essentials into the priority area, they must be labelled urgent. This labelling exercise is a simple trick, but it produces wonderful results.

Delegation and Time Management

Learning how to delegate will help you save time, and at the same time motivate and train your employees. In this way you will be able to achieve more without burning yourself out. It is also a first step in training your assistants and free up time to take on new responsibilities in order to grow your business.

There are three main concepts that should guide your delegation process: (1) authority, (2) responsibility, and (3) accountability. Remember that when you delegate you share authority with the employee to whom you have delegated a particular task. Authority is the power you give to the employee to act and make decisions within designated boundaries. Responsibility refers to the act of carrying out the task. When delegating a task, you share the responsibility of completing the work with the employee to whom you have delegated the task. Your responsibility is to provide clear-cut instructions on what work needs to be done, while your employee is responsible for figuring out how the task should be completed. During delegation of a task, the accountability of the task transfers from you to your employee. Accountability here is the act of being liable for one's actions and decisions.

The first step in the delegation process is to carefully select which task to delegate. Not every task is an ideal candidate to delegate. Some of the tasks that are placed in quadrant III may be considered for delegation. The second step is to choose the right persons to perform the tasks. This step can be one of the hardest steps. It takes time and effort to find a person who possesses all the traits and skills required for the job. The person not only needs to have the right technical skills or expert knowledge, but also needs to be trustworthy and have the time to take on the additional work. In addition, the person needs to have similar values and ethics to the person delegating the task. The next step in the delegation process is to monitor the progress of the knowledge and skill transfer. Regularly follow-up on how well the person is completing the work. Initially, you will spend some time in the monitoring process and make yourself available for questions and provide feedback on the progress of the work to guarantee the delegation process is successfully completed. But once the employee has mastered the tasks, you will free yourself up for tasks that are both urgent and important.

Chapter Thirteen

Putting Your Customers at the Centre of Your Decisions

Introduction

Customer-centrism became a popular buzz word in business magazines in the 1980s and 1990s and is still extensively used to date. A customer-centric approach to business management simply means that the customer is at the centre of all decisions that managers and employees take and the manner in which they behave towards customers. This business philosophy is also described as *market orientation* in academic literature. Market-oriented companies tend to develop business cultures that depend on organisation-wide learning systems. It means all employees continuously learn and reflect or their daily interactions with their customers and share these experiences with other employees through well-organised systems of information generation and sharing. In some companies, the degrees of customer-orientation shown by employees in their interactions with customers are measured, and employees who show higher degrees of customer orientation are rewarded accordingly. This means, if your company is very customer-oriented, it will have sustainable advantage over its immediate competitors.

This chapter shows you how customer orientation can help you develop a strong business management culture that can enhance the performance of your company for many years. The chapter begins with an outline of typical customer expectations and the dominant characteristics of a market-oriented company in general. We also introduce you to another set of popular concepts in business strategy – i.e. Red Ocean and Blue Ocean strategies. Thus, the chapter provides you with a new set of business vocabularies that can help you think through your business strategies.

Customer Expectations

Expectation can be defined as product characteristics and the level of service the customer hopes to receive. It is a "wished for" level – i.e. a combination of what customers believe can and should be delivered in the context of their personal needs. The marketing literature refers to this as a desirable expectation – i.e. reflections of the hopes and wishes of customers. The desirable expectation may also be termed *ideal expectation* – i.e. an expectation of what "perfect" service should be.

However, most customers are realistic and appreciate the fact that companies may not be able to deliver the desired level of service each time, hence they have a tolerance level or "threshold" level of expectations. This is referred to in the marketing literature as the "zone of tolerance" or "adequate service level" – i.e. the range of service performance that customers consider satisfactory. In other words, they may accept some performance variation within that mentally defined range.

When customers select a product or a company to deliver the services that they need, they will normally have a prediction of what level of service they are likely to receive based on either of two sets of information/knowledge or a combination of both:

1. Prior experience of customers with a specific service provider, with competing service providers in the same industry, or with related services in different industries.

2. If they have no relevant prior experiences, customers may base their pre-purchase expectation on word-of-mouth comments, news stories, or the service provider's own marketing efforts (mass and non-mass media communication).

Marketing scholars argue that most customers have the following five key expectations from products and services they consider buying:

1. Nature of Products and Services: Customers expect the products and services they are offered to be appropriate to their needs. The size and frequency of purchase may influence the type of products or services customers consider to be appropriate. A customer that makes a small, spontaneous purchase does not expect the same level of service as one that makes a large purchase or frequent purchases.

2. Price: The cost of everything we purchase is becoming more and more important since everyone wants to use his financial resources as efficiently as possible.

3. Quality: Customers want the products that they purchase to be durable and functional. Even perishable items should last long enough for them to be used without loss of value. Food items must be of a quality that does not endanger the health of the users. There is a psychological relationship between price and quality. Most customers consider it fair for companies to charge relatively higher prices for items deemed to be of superior quality than similar items from competitors.

4. Action: Customers are human beings and like to think that they are as important as any other person. They therefore expect action when a problem or question arises – i.e. someone will be ready to assist them when a problem arises.

5. Appreciation: Customers need to know that employees of companies from which they buy appreciate their money. Saying thank you to the customer through our words and actions is a good starting point.

Box 13-1

Treat your Customers as Members of a Royal Family

Your customers are your kings, queens, princes and princesses. They are also your employers. It is because of your customers that your businesses exist. They expect you to make them feel this way. If any of your key customers defect to a competitor, he leaves with a chain of others; if he remains, he brings in a chain of other customers.

Market-Orientation and Blue Ocean Strategy

These expectations must be fulfilled by a market-oriented company and its employees. As indicated in the introduction to this chapter, market-oriented companies are those that are highly sensitive to the needs of their customers and proactively take steps to fulfil these needs. Market-oriented companies have other defining characteristics. First, they are capable of responding quickly to competitor challenges and are able to spot any evidence of customer dissatisfaction. Second, they are also able to quickly detect changes in customer needs and product preferences and take the necessary actions in response to the information. Third, they are also effective in getting all business functions to work together to provide superior customer value.

In 2005, W. Chan Kim and Renée Mauborgne from INSEAD published the book *Blue Ocean Strategy - How to Create Uncontested Market Space and Make Competition Irrelevant*. It quickly became a best seller because it provided a new strategic direction to many managers. They also popularised the concept of value innovation in that publication. Their argument is that market orientation alone cannot guarantee business success and growth. They describe those companies that strive to succeed in existing market space as adopting "red ocean" strategies – i.e. they serve existing demand. In contrast the more successful companies adopt "blue ocean" strategies. In blue oceans, demand is created rather than fought over, and there is ample opportunity for growth.

Kim and Mauborgne offer the following guidelines to companies in the blue ocean strategy formulation process:

1. **Do not** compete in existing market space, **instead** you should create uncontested market space.

2. **Do not** beat the competition, **instead** you should make the competition irrelevant.

3. **Do not** exploit existing demand, **instead** you should create and capture new demand.

4. **Do not** make the value/cost trade-off, **instead** you should break the value/cost trade-off.

5. **Do not** align the whole system of a company's activities with its strategic choice of differentiation or low cost, **instead** you should align the whole system of a company's activities in pursuit of both differentiation and low cost

The Role of Employees in Making Customers Happy

As hinted earlier, it is the frontline employees that influence customers' perceptions of a service company's responsiveness to their needs. They do so through their personal willingness to go the 'extra mile' to serve their customers (or annoy them with their bad work attitude). This means that whether or not a customer perceives a company as delivering the service promised depends on the attitude, commitment and behaviour of service employees. The management literature shows that work attitude is partly shaped by organisational culture. This means a customer service environment should have a customer service-oriented culture.

Managing Customer Complaints

You must expect occasional mistakes in your service delivery process, no matter how well your employees try. A customer may accidentally be overcharged for service, there may be power outage, your inputs supplier may disappoint you or a frontline employee may have a bad day. Customer complaint is, therefore, not entirely avoidable. Your responsibility as a service provider is to respond to the customer's complaints in a manner that increases satisfaction. Even though complaints may sometimes seem undesirable, they nevertheless serve as a source of important feedback for your company. They contain the direct voice of the customer. If complaints are transformed into knowledge about customers, they can provide a valuable amount of goodwill for your company. A bank teller for example, has no business snapping at a customer if the customer complains about the long wait he has had to endure before he got served. The customer's complaint is a free message to the bank that service might be too slow and customers may be uncomfortable about it. Complaining customers could be the most loyal customers of your company, if their complaints are well handled. Your company must, therefore, design, build, operate and continuously upgrade systems for managing complaints. These systems are called customer complaint management systems (CCMS).

Chapter Fourteen

Highlights and Reflections

Introduction

My aim in this book is to give some practical guidelines to those of you who already have businesses or are contemplating establishing businesses in Ghana. I believe that if you follow these guidelines your chances of being successful will be greatly enhanced over time. This final chapter summarises the main points I have presented above.

Highlights

To begin it all you must assess your personal capabilities as an entrepreneur before plunging into business. Entering business out of necessity does not ensure success. You must also make a realistic assessment of the demands that the entrepreneurial role will make on you and your family. Furthermore, you must evaluate your managerial skills and conduct a personal financial assessment. These assessments will keep your business perspective in a sharper focus and guide you as to what you need to do from the onset in order to succeed.

I have argued further that your mindset is the first key to your success. It is often said that entrepreneurs are driven by an immense desire to achieve the goals they initially set for themselves and then to aim for even more challenging standards. The competitive needs of growth-minded entrepreneurs are to outperform their own previous best results, rather than just to outperform another person. In other words, be action-oriented. Successful entrepreneurs are therefore described more as "doers" rather than "dreamers". They are action-oriented people; they want to start producing results immediately. They are not intimidated by the number or severity of the problems they encounter. In fact, their self-confidence and general optimism seem to translate into a view that nothing is impossible in business – goals may sometimes just take a little longer to achieve. They will work with a stubborn tenacity to solve a difficult problem.

Unlike most people, entrepreneurs do not allow themselves to be concerned with failure. They do not think so much about what they are going to do if they do not make it. They rather focus their thoughts and energy on what they have to do to succeed.

The starting point is the determination within us to nurture our potentials and to bring about a real change. When the determination is there, everything else begins to move in the direction that we desire. The moment you resolve to be an achiever, every nerve and fibre within your body immediately orients itself towards your success. I have also suggested that you should not aim at making money merely for the sake of being rich. You must make profits for a purpose. If you agree with the view that the primary determinant of meaning in life is other people, then you must see your business goals as being closely linked with a desire to create value and make life meaningful for you and other people in Ghana and beyond. See money as a tool for creating that higher level value in society. With this focus you will develop an inner motivation and tenacity to weather the storms of building a viable business and designing a winning strategy. A winning strategy requires you to pay careful attention equally to both efficiency and effectiveness in your business activities. You will also be willing to develop trust with your business partners as well as other stakeholders in your business circles. A winning strategy also entails managing your employees well and choosing an appropriate leadership style. To do this effectively you must communicate with maturity, engage in fast learning, generate positive human energy, and manage your time effectively. Finally, you must always remember to put your customers at the centre of your decisions. See your customers as your kings, queens, princes and princesses. They are also your employers. It is because of your customers that your business exists. They expect you to make them feel this way. If any of your key customers defects to a competitor, he leaves with a chain of others; if he remains, he brings in a chain of other customers.

Treat your employees as if they are your customers. In fact they are your marketing service providers. If they are satisfied, they will be committed to your company and they will want you to succeed because their own success depends on your success. Your employees must therefore be motivated.

There are a number of things you must do or must not do when dealing with your employees. For example, never use threats when dealing with them. They will feel displeased, uncommitted and even turn people against you. This does not mean that you should not make them aware of the negative consequences of not getting the results you want in your company. It rather means that you must communicate your expectations in positive and inspiring manner. Setting inspiring expectations is the most certain way of creating eager and productive employees. But be specific in your communication. If you want a specific result, give specific instructions. People work better when they know exactly what is expected of them. It also means that if any of your employees is doing something wrong let the person know. Most people want to improve and will make an effort once they know how to do it.

You must also remember that all human beings can be motivated by appealing to their selfish nature. If you give your employees the opportunity to earn more personally they will earn more for you as well.

You must also make a point to show acknowledgement and appreciation of achievements of your employees within your company and in their personal life. This will make them feel that you are paying attention and see them as individuals and not just "human resources". All people like to see that their efforts are not being ignored.

You must also try as much as you can to create a team spirit among your employees. People tend to work more effectively when they feel like part of a team — they don't want to let others down. This holds true for Ghanaian workers as well.

Empowerment is an important source of motivation. You must therefore allow your key employees to make decisions in matters that they have personal expertise. Focus on results and do not micro-manage every action taken in your company.

This means you must treat mistakes and failures as temporary setbacks on the way to accomplishing your goals. Unlike most people, the bruises of the defeats of growth-oriented business people heal quickly. They have the ability to come to terms with their mistakes, learn from them, correct them, and use them to prevent their recurrence. This allows them to return to the business world again soon after their failure.

Be a disciplined person when it comes to finances. What makes businesses grow is not so much how much you earn but how much of your earnings you save and plough back into the company. This means you must keep your business accounts separate from your personal accounts. Develop a personal balance sheet and a personal budget. The bitterest experiences of many Ghanaian entrepreneurs have to do with mixing business finances with personal finances. Keep yourself on a salary and maintain a modest life style while your business is growing.

Financial discipline has an added advantage; it will enable you to get financial support from banks and other financial institutions. Your personal balance sheet provides potential lenders with a view of your overall financial situation so they can assess the risk they will be assuming. This means, if you are in a strong financial position, you will be considered a desirable prospect.

Look far Ahead2

As a closing remark, remember that we see things the way our minds have instructed our eyes to see them. Thus, your first challenge in growing your business is to change your mindset. Look far ahead into the future – not two year but two or three decades. You may even see your business growth beyond your own life time. With such a long term orientation you will see any failures you might experience as just temporary and continue to fight on.

Bibliography

Assimeng, Max (1981) *Social Structure of Ghana* (AccraGhana Publishing Corporation)

Berne, Eric (1964) *Games people play: The psychology of human relationships* (New York: Grove Press)

Covey, S.R, (1989) *The 7 Habits of Highly Effective People* (New York, Simon & Schuster)

Covey, S.R, Merrill, A.R, (1994) *First Things First*, (New York, Simon & Schuster)

Dweck, Carol (2006) *Mindset: The New Psychology of Success* (New York Ballantine Books)

Elkington, J. (2004) Enter the triple bottom line, Chapter 1 of Henriques, A. and Richardson, J, (eds) *The Triple Bottom Line: Does It All Add Up*? (London, Earthscan Publications) Available at http://kmhassociates.ca/resources/1/Triple%20Bottom %20Line%20a%20history%201961- 2001.pdf.

Fukuyama, Francis (1995) *Trust: The Social Virtues and the Creation of Prosperity* (NY. A Free Press)

Hart, S. and London, T. (2005) "Developing native capability: What multinational corporations can learn from the base of the pyramid", *Stanford Social Innovation Review*, Summer: 28-33.

Hersey, Paul (2007) *Management of Organizational behavior*, (Ninth edition, Upper Saddle River)

Johnson, David W. (1993) *Reaching Out* 5th Edition (Boston, Allyn and Bacon)

Kim, W. Chan and Mauborgne, Renée (2005) *Blue Ocean Strategy - How to Create Uncontested Market Space and Make Competition Irrelevant* (Boston, Harvard Business School Press)

Kotler, P. and Lee, N., (2009) *Up and Out of Poverty: The Social Marketing Solution* (Upper Saddle River, NJ: Wharton School Publishing)

Kuada, John (2016A) *Global Mindsets: Exploration and Perspectives* (London, Routledge)

Kuada, John (2016B) *Marketing Decisions and Strategies: An International Perspective* (London: Adonis & Abbey Publishers Ltd.)

Lim, Siong Guan and Joanne H. Lim (2014) *The Leader, The Teacher and You* (London, Imperial College Press)

Maxwell, John (2007) *Failing Forward: Turning Mistakes into Stepping Stones for Success* (Nashville, Thomas Nelson Inc.)

McKinsey Global Institute (2010) *Lions on the move: The progress and potential of African economies* (McKinsey Company) Available at http://www.adlevocapital.com/images/Lions_on_the_ Move.pdf Accessed on 15- 11- 2012

Millman, Debbie (2007) *How to Think Like A Great Graphic Designer* (New York, Allworth Press)

Prahalad, C. K. (2005) *The Fortune at the Bottom of the Pyramid: Eradicating Poverty through Profits.* (Upper Saddle River, NJ: Prentice Hall)

Prahalad C.K. and G. Hamel (1990) "The Core Competence of Corporations" *Harvard Business Review* Vol. 66 May/June pp: 79-91

INDEX

www.ingramcontent.com/pod-product-compliance
Lightning Source LLC
Chambersburg PA
CBHW071607200326

41519CB00021BB/6904